DATE DUE

Praise for *Silicon Dragon*

"With fine writing flair and investigative footwork, Rebecca Fannin unveils the pullulating panorama of the Chinese tech menagerie, replete with yapping yahoos!, google-raptors, repli-cats and Shanghai sili-manders—all the fierce but finally friendly dragons blowing out much smoke amid their bolts of inventive flame that make China the most fateful and fascinating entrepreneurial story of the 21st century. I'm a Fannin fan."

George Gilder
editor-in-chief, *Gilder Technology Report*
chairman, Gilder Publishing
senior fellow, Discovery Institute

"China is on its way to becoming the economic superpower, and it is only a matter of time before it starts to flex its muscle in the technology industry. It is already setting its own telecom standards and is building an unrivaled broadband infrastructure. It is going to be the next big bed of innovation, and *Silicon Dragon* will give you a road map for this new brave world."

Om Malik
author, *Broadbandits: Inside the $750 Billion Telecom Heist*
founder and senior writer, technology blog GigaOM

"Rebecca Fannin's *Silicon Dragon* provides an insightful view of the unique entrepreneurial environment in China and profiles some of its most accomplished entrepreneurs. She explains why China is and is likely to continue to be a country that provides the highest returns on venture capital investing."

Patrick J. McGovern
founder and chairman
International Data Group

"China's emergence as a technological giant is among the most interesting and important subjects in business and economics. Yet China remains a mystery to most Western technology observers. Rebecca Fannin performs an invaluable service in explaining and detailing China's growth into the tech engine of the 21st century."

Jason Pontin
editor-in-chief and publisher, *Technology Review*
columnist, *The New York Times*

"*Silicon Dragon* presents a unique and well-reported look into the rapid ascent of Chinese entrepreneurs and venture capitalists who are defining the frontiers of global technology. A 'high-five' to Ms. Fannin who took the the time in Beijing, Shanghai and the Valley to tell their story to the world."

Dan Schwartz
chairman and publisher
Asian Venture Capital Journal

SILICON DRAGON

HOW CHINA IS WINNING THE TECH RACE

REBECCA A. FANNIN

Mc
Graw
Hill

New York   Chicago   San Francisco   Lisbon   London
Madrid   Mexico City   Milan   New Delhi   San Juan   Seoul
Singapore   Sydney   Toronto

ISBN: 978 0-07-149447-2
MHID 0-07-149447-2

McGraw-Hill books are available at special quantity discounts to use as premiums and sales promotions, or for use in corporate training programs. To contact a representative please visit the Contact Us pages at www.mhprofessional.com.

This book is printed on recycled, acid-free paper containing a minimum of 50% recycled, de-inked fiber.

All photos are reproduced and copyright courtesy of the author, Rebecca Fannin, with the following exceptions: Chapter 1, courtesy Nasdaq, Chapter 7, courtesy *Asian Venture Capital Journal*. All rights are reserved.

Library of Congress Cataloging-in-Publication Data

Fannin, Rebecca A.
  Silicon dragon / by Rebecca A. Fannin.
     p. cm.
  ISBN-13: 978-0-07-149447-2
  MHID 0-07-149447-2
  1. Internet industry--China. 2. High technology industries--China. 3. Information technology--China. I. Title.
  HD9696.8.C62F36 2008
  338.0951--dc22   2007048293

To my family, both near and far

c o n t e n t s

Introduction - XI

PART ONE

The Copycats

Chapter One - 3
Baidu—China's Boldest Internet Start-Up
Robin Li took what he learned in Silicon Valley to beat Google in China and become a multimillionaire. But he almost didn't make it in the early days.

Chapter Two - 19
Alibaba—The Wizardry of Jack Ma
Not even Harry Potter's author could imagine a tale as magical as Jack Ma's: He beat eBay and Yahoo! in China and scored a record IPO.

Chapter Three - 33
Dangdang.com—The Amazon Plus of China
Cofounder Peggy YuYu has shown how to copy and then outsmart Amazon.com in China. Watch out Jeff Bezos.

Chapter Four - 45
Chinacars.com—Cruisin' with Style
John Zhang has modernized the all-American AAA brand down to its name—CCC—in China's zooming car market. Next stop, Nasdaq.

Chapter Five - 57
Oak Pacific Interactive—Web 2.0 on Steroids
Joe Chen created copies of MySpace, YouTube, Facebook, and Craigslist. With Murdoch at the door and losses to contend with, his survival skills are in for a test.

Chapter Six - **7 1**

Bokee.com—Growing Pains

Free speech crusader Fang Xingdong coined the Chinese term for blogging and set up China's first blog service, but he got booted as CEO, and his site may not survive.

PART TWO

The Venture Capitalists

Chapter Seven - **85**

Silicon Valley's Tech Route to China

Leading American venture capitalists are searching for deals and the next new thing in Beijing, Shanghai, Hangzhou, and beyond. But will the rush yield poor returns?

PART THREE

The Innovators

The next five profiles of Chinese tech entrepreneurs show the rise of China as an innovator, not just a copier of American ideas.

Chapter Eight - **1 0 1**

Lingtu—China's Navigator

This local team put maps of the Three Gorges dam, the Olympics site, and Mount Everest on mobile phones, in cars, on CDs, and on the Web, but it turned outside for a CEO.

Chapter Nine - **1 1 3**

Oriental Wisdom—Confucian Capitalism

First-time entrepreneur Liu Yingkui has invented software for selling financial goods over cell phones, not PCs. Now he needs to get to the next level.

Chapter Ten - **1 2 3**

Pingco—Ping Me, Please

Move over Skype. Here comes PingCo and short text messages by mobile phone for free. It's a technology that could go global, if China Mobile doesn't kill it.

Chapter Eleven - **1 3 3**

Maxthon—The Way China Surfs the World

Jeff Chen has signed up more than 100 million users for his innovative Web browser Maxthon, attracted Google as an investor, and has Microsoft on the alert.

Chapter Twelve - **143**

LatticePower Corporation—China Lights Up the Globe

Chinese scientist Jiang Fengyi could be the next Thomas Edison. He already has 15 patents for making high-tech lights.

Endnotes - **153**

Acknowledgments - **167**

Index - **171**

SILICON DRAGON

HOW CHINA IS WINNING THE TECH RACE

i n t r o d u c t i o n

I t's a sunny Sunday afternoon on a rare smog-free day in Shanghai, an ideal time to stroll in one of the city's new urban parks. But in China, business still comes before leisure, sunshine or not. At a popular diner called Element Fresh in Shanghai's Huaihai Zhong Lu shopping district, the steel tabletop is strewn with plates of half-eaten noodles and soup, used chopsticks, and half-empty cups. No one cares about the mess.

Dressed in a bright orange jacket with spiky hair colored to match, Gary Wang clicks on his Web site, uploads a video, downloads another one, and chats online, all the while making a classic so-called elevator pitch for funding. Helen Wong nods, listening attentively. A petite and perky but determined venture capitalist, she's just moved to Shanghai and can't wait to do her first deal in red-hot China. A few weeks later Gary has $8.5 million[1] in hand from Helen's firm. He's anxious to ramp up Tudou.com, China's first and leading video-sharing service; it's a lot like YouTube.com, which had its U.S. debut about the same time in a Silicon Valley garage. "New technologies in China are happening almost simultaneously, almost instantaneously with the United States," he says.

East-West tech culture

In the mid-1990s, at the height of the Internet bubble, a coffee shop called Buck's in upscale Woodside, California, was the epicenter of innovation, the place where business plans were scribbled on napkins and start-ups were seeded.

Today the compass has shifted eastward to China. The Carlyle Group, a Washington, D.C.–based private equity firm, has wasted no time in investing in the China tech rush, says David Rubenstein, Carlyle's cofounder: "The center of technology is shifting, and China is emerging as the other major pole for innovation."

Zhongguancun Software Park is in a distant northwestern corner of Beijing, on the way to the ancient Summer Palace of Chinese emperors. The modern office park is one of several new bustling high-tech and science zones and is home to some 12,000 small businesses. The sprawling district feeds off engineering and business graduates from China's top-tier Tsinghua University and Beijing University, just as Stanford University grads helped transform California's Silicon Valley from fertile agricultural land to Tech Central 30 years ago. Len Baker, a boyish 64-year-old partner at the venture capital firm that funded Oracle Corp., Sutter Hill Ventures, is mining for start-up gems in China. "China is where Silicon Valley was three decades ago when several high-tech companies got their start," he declares.

The in thing among bright young Chinese techies is to draw up a business plan, get financing, scale the start-up to sizable revenues and profits, and then go public in the United States. An army of so-called technopreneurs like Wang are turbocharging world-class enterprises. Call them collectively a new rival to the Valley's tech dominance, or Silicon Dragon.

A rising supply of tech talent and surplus capital is feeding the dragon.[2] Thousands of Western-educated and -trained young Chinese—the first generation to study and work abroad since Chinese communism began in 1949—have returned to their homeland with advanced degrees and Valley entrepreneurial know-how to crank up businesses. The reforms of former leader Deng Xiaoping and his frequently quoted 1992 phrase "to get rich is glorious" unleashed change, and tech entrepreneurship has proved to be a golden path to cashing in.

There's still a lack of managerial and leadership experience at many Chinese tech start-ups that puts them at a competitive disadvantage in building successful enterprises, observes Kyung Yoon, vice chairman of the recruiting firm Heidrick & Struggles.[3] But there's no shortage of technical talent on the Mainland. As many as 644,000 engineers—three times more than in the United States[4]—graduate annually from Chinese universities.

Investments in Chinese start-ups surged 28 percent to $6.8 billion in 2006—about one-third of the $22 billion that went to all Asian start-ups—and added another $3 billion in the first half of 2007, compared with only $335 million in 2002.[5] China remains tiny next to the dominant U.S. market, but it has been the world's fastest-growing venture capital market for several years in a row (see Table 1).[6]

Boosted by low operating costs, booming consumer demand in the newly capitalistic economy, and 9.5 percent-plus economic growth for two decades, Chinese start-ups are scaling up and reaching profitability at lightning speed. Listed Chinese Internet players show high operating margins of 28

> *"Chinese entrepreneurs make the United States look like it needs steroids."*
>
> **Jim Breyer,**
> managing partner, Accel Partners

percent, almost twice as high as those of their U.S. peers.[7] Chinacars.com, an online version of the American AAA automotive club, launched in 2001, is only one example. It topped $13 million in revenues and $2 million in profits

	2002*	2003	2004	2005	2006	2007 (first half)
China	$335	1,602	1,427	4,943	6,794	3,045
Asia	$3,004	3,261	3,127	8,282	22,192	8,460
United States**	$21,059	18,827	21,671	23,490	26,359	14,132

*All figures are in $ millions.
**U.S. figures include later-stage start-ups.
Source: For Asia: *Asian Venture Capital Journal*; for United States, Dow Jones VentureOne.

**Table 1 Venture Capital Flows into China
Amount Invested in Start-ups**

in just three years, CEO and founder John Zhang tells me in his loft-style office with a distant view of the Forbidden City, the former Chinese Imperial Palace now at the heart of modern Beijing.

Jim Breyer is the savvy managing partner of Accel Partners and a backer of the popular social networking site Facebook. "Chinese entrepreneurs make the United States look like it needs steroids," he says.

The Chinese technology revolution is as unstoppable as a locomotive. Today over 65 Chinese companies trade on Nasdaq and the New York Stock Exchange. As recently as 1999, none did. Thirty-one made their U.S. public debut in 2006 and the first half of 2007 (see Table 2).

Moreover, nine Chinese tech firms reached market capitalizations of $1 billion, and four surpassed $3 billion in 2006. Not bad compared with the United States, which had only one tech firm pass the $1 billion mark in 2005.[8]

IPOs ON NASDAQ			IPOs ON THE NEW YORK STOCK EXCHANGE		
	China[1]	Total[2]		China	Total
2000[3]	7	391	2000	3	49
2001	8	63	2001	2	39
2002	6	51	2002	1	41
2003	7	56	2003	1	30
2004	16	170	2004	2	80
2005	24	139	2005	1	71
2006	34	137	2006	3	66
2007[4]	46[5]	142	First half 2007	6	34

[1]Number of Chinese companies listed on Nasdaq by year end. [2]Total refers to U.S. and overseas companies. [3]Cumulative figures. [4]As of July 27, 2007. [5]As of March 3, 2007.

Source: New York Stock Exchange.

Table 2 Chinese IPOs Gain on U.S. Exchanges

"It adds up to a tipping point for U.S. dominance of technology," says Richard Lim, a Beijing-based managing director with GSR Ventures (see Table 3).

Adding to the momentum, tech firms increasingly are going public in Shanghai and Hong Kong. The markets are sizzling. The number of stock market investors in China reached nearly 100 million by mid-2007 as cab drivers, housewives, and retirees raced to get rich. This is remarkable considering that China reopened local exchanges only in 1991 after the communist victory of 1949 had shut them down.

Today's China is switched on. The Middle Kingdom has the world's largest number of mobile phone users (500 million), the second-largest number of Internet users (162 million), and 2 of the top 10 Web sites globally.[9] China accounts for 24 percent of world production of semiconductors—silicon chips that make electronic devices work—and is projected to have one-third of the global market by 2010.[10] Chinese chipmakers such as the NYSE-listed Semiconductor Manufacturing International Corp. in Shanghai's Pudong industrial area already make 7 percent of the world's chips.

Chinese goods once stood for cheap knockoffs found in Wal-Mart and, more recently, for tainted imports, but with the Internet revolution, a tipping point took hold. Young Chinese "returnees," so-called sea turtles, began churning out close imitations of successful U.S. dot-coms and tweaking them with local characteristics that no American multinational, eBay, Google, and Yahoo! included, could get exactly right. Among the Chinese transplants, which were funded largely by American venture investors, were copies of

TOTAL CAPITALIZATION OF NASDAQ COMPANIES		TOTAL CAPITALIZATION OF NASDAQ-LISTED CHINESE COMPANIES	
2005	$3,846.7 billion[1]	2005	$14.5 billion[3]
2006	$4,132.6 billion	2006	$23.6 billion
2007[2]	$4,503.9 billion	2007[4]	$39.9 billion

[1]Combined U.S. market cap. [2]As of June 30, 2007. [3]Combined global market cap. [4]As of July 27, 2007.

Source: Nasdaq.

Table 3 Chinese IPOs Going Strong

Google, eBay, MySpace, and Amazon. Other early related by-products of that process are Lenovo personal computers, Haier appliances, and Huawei electronics goods: Chinese brand names that have emerged globally.

Today, a fresh generation of homegrown super-innovators is replacing the master duplicators. Chinese whiz kids, more often than not funded by domestic venture capital firms, are coming up with cutting-edge advances for cell phones, chips, e-commerce, and software at the same time as and often ahead of the West. Paul Saffo, a Silicon Valley tech forecaster,[11] likens China's progress from copycats to innovators to the Swiss copying American watch-making methods at the turn of the twentieth century and then developing the world's best watches. "The pattern is the same, going after the low-hanging fruit and then becoming more innovative," he says. "When I go to China and visit a high-tech firm, I look around and ask, Which one of these people will be the next Steve Jobs?"

In 2006, China chalked up the world's fastest growth rate for new patent applications, a 56 percent increase to 3,910,[12] ranking it eighth globally, although it is still far behind the U.S. number of nearly 51,000 patent applications (see Table 4).

INTERNATIONAL PATENT APPLICATIONS

	2002	2003	2004	2005	2006	% Change
United States	41,296	41,029	43,350	46,772	50,089	7.1
China	1,018	1,295	1,706	2,499	3,910	56.5

Source: World Intellectual Property Organization.

PATENTS GRANTED IN CHINA

1985–2002	2003	2004	2005	2006
792,352	149,588	151,328	171,619	223,860

Source: State Intellectual Property Office of the People's Republic of China.

Table 4 Applications Rise for Patents in China

The gains are driven in part by the Chinese government's latest five-year plan and President Hu Jintao's pledge to make high-tech innovation the cornerstone of economic growth and social development and the main source of wealth in the twenty-first century. Dr. Robert Lawrence Kuhn, an informal adviser to the Chinese government[13] says, "Technology is being looked at as an economic driver and a force to develop a harmonious society that can deal with the growing imbalances of rich and poor and other social ills such as pollution and perhaps even corruption."

Creativity behind the Great Wall was suppressed by the Cultural Revolution and authoritarian Communist Party rule, yet the Chinese have long had innate inventive talent. They gave the world paper, gunpowder, the calculator (i.e., the abacus), and the compass, not to mention Chinese medicine, Confucian philosophy, and finely woven silk cloth.

Chinese whiz kids

Liu Yingkui, who goes by the name "King," is one of the new innovators in today's China. Over drinks in a Beijing bar, King excitedly tells me in broken English that his company, Oriental Wisdom, makes advanced software for customer sales management. It works on mobile phones, not personal computers, as more common in the United States. At his obscure office in the HaiDian high-tech and university district of Beijing, Jeff Chen demonstrates an Internet browser called Maxthon that has Microsoft scurrying to adapt some of its features for Internet Explorer. Near the gates of Tsinghua University, Charles Wang introduces me to PingCo, one of the world's first free instant messaging services for mobile phones. On the campus of Nanchang University in southeastern China, Professor Jiang Fengyi, founder of LatticePower Corporation, shows me how he is cranking out lights that promise to replace the standard General Electric bulbs. Over a Chinese box lunch at his Shanghai high-rise headquarters, Shi Zhengrong, chairman and CEO of NYSE-listed Suntech Power Holdings,[14] tells me that he holds 11 patents for producing lower-cost solar panels with silicon. I later visit Suntech's plant in smoggy industrialized Wuxi that is making electricity from sunlight. Six-year-old Suntech is on track to double 2007 revenues to $1.2 billion and become the world's third largest solar energy producer. Today Shi is the seventh richest person in China and the 432nd in the world with a self-made fortune of $2.2 billion.[15]

China is leapfrogging past a legacy of outdated formats that stymie Western firms. Because of the size and stature of China's markets, such innovations could set world standards for technology. In turn, Western companies will have to adapt or outperform to compete. Look what happened to Detroit back in the 1970s when Japanese compact cars arrived.

It's a transformation of historical proportions, comparable to the Industrial Revolution. For years global economists have been predicting that China soon will be the world's largest economy and a superpower. Ohio State University professor and China expert Oded Shenkar[16] concludes that the United States is vulnerable to the Mainland's ascent as China infuses modern technology and market economics into a nondemocratic, communist-controlled system.

> "The Net for China is like the steam engine for Europe and the automobile for the United States."
>
> **Edward Tian,**
> founder and chairman,
> Broadband Capital Partners

"In China, the role model was Chairman Mao, and now it's Jack Ma," says Edward Tian, a venture capitalist at Broadband Capital Partners and vice chairman of formerly state-owned China Netcom. He's referring to the charismatic leader of the e-commerce start-up Alibaba.com, which recently went public in a record-breaking initial public offering. Alibaba.com received a $1 billion investment from Yahoo! in 2005 and then took over the operation of Yahoo! China. "China missed the last Industrial Revolution, but we won't miss this one," promises Tian, who founded AsiaInfo, the first Chinese tech firm to go public on Nasdaq. "The Net for China is like the steam engine for Europe and the automobile for the United States."

China's ills

China still faces enormous challenges: income inequality, horrendous air and water pollution, bloated state-owned enterprises, bad bank loans, and social instability. The long list of hurdles includes illiquid domestic stock exchanges, a nonconvertible currency, lack of financial transparency, abrupt shifts in regulatory policy, complex requirements for foreign investors, and lack of enforcement against makers of counterfeit goods. Those obstacles have convinced Yahoo!'s cofounder and CEO Jerry Yang that, "It will be another 15 to 20 years before China develops the infrastructure to challenge the United States for technology leadership."

Even then it may not develop the distinct innovative and entrepreneurial edge that Silicon Valley's ecosystem has spawned in multiple high-tech areas, says Marguerite Hancock, associate director of the Stanford Project on Regions of Innovation and Entrepreneurship. Most of the innovation coming out of China is centered on processes or business model innovation, not disruptive technology that breaks the mold, she points out. "I think it's too early to tell if China can compete in the same league."

Silicon Valley commentator Tony Perkins, head of the blogging network AlwaysOn and founder of *Red Herring* and *Upside* tech magazines, suggests that China does not have the right cultural environment to encourage innovation. He cites lack of democracy, censorship, weak intellectual property protection, and lack of freedom of the press as forces that stifle creativity in the Middle Kingdom. "My personal view is that China is long-term handicapped and has to have fundamental cultural change to be a serious competitive threat," he says.

"Before any cutting-edge innovations in China can develop," adds Beijing tech consultant Mark Natkin, "there needs to be a fundamental change in the educational system to encourage risk taking and innovation from day one."

To be sure, China claims a small fraction of the world's tech innovations today. But in the next two decades it will account for about one-quarter of the world's new tech ideas, notes David Chao, cofounder and general partner of DCM, whose portfolio includes several Nasdaq-listed Chinese companies. As

China rises, Chao claims, it will cut into the commanding 90 percent global share of U.S. technological advances in the Internet, personal computers, and cell phones. "It will only be 10 to 20 years before China sees the likes of Gates or Jobs," he says.

The next new thing

No wonder top-tier Valley venture capitalists such as Sequoia Capital and Kleiner Perkins Caufield & Byers are racking up frequent-flier miles to China to sniff out the next Google, Skype, or Hotmail. Just a few years ago those titans rarely drove beyond a 30-mile radius from their homes in Atherton, Hillsborough, and Woodside in San Mateo County, California.

Friends and family members used to be the only source of cash for start-up businesses. Today Chinese entrepreneurs pick venture firms that offer the best financial terms and the most connections. The lobbies of the Four Seasons Hotel in Shanghai and the Grand Hyatt in Beijing are popular meeting points for negotiating deals. So are regular networking parties at trendy spots such as the Museum of Contemporary Art in People's Park. They remind me of the freewheeling party scene in Silicon Valley in the late 1990s. But even though some expect China's bubble to burst soon, China's tech economy is here to stay. Venture capital still accounts for a comparatively tiny portion of the overall Chinese economy,[17] and the boom is expected to keep going for another 20 to 30 years.

The wide-open opportunities in China have little in common with the ill-fated joint ventures made by pioneer investors in the People's Republic of China some 15 years earlier. Many experienced China investors, such as Ta-lin Hsu of the private equity firm H&Q Asia Pacific, were tripped up by corruption and fraud and barely earned a *renminbi*, the Chinese currency, from their initial investments. Today venture capital is hip. Hsu's son Mark, who works for his dad, hangs out with Brazilian models and was, until he got married, labeled Shanghai's most eligible bachelor. A reality TV show about entrepreneurship, *Win in China*, airs on state-owned China Central Television and is modeled on *The Apprentice*. Entrepreneurs pitch their business ideas before a panel of judges from China's corporate elite, and the winners get prize money up to $1.3 million for their start-ups. The money is put up by the well-known local venture capitalists Andrew Yan, Kathy Xu, and Hugo Shong, who take a 50 percent stake in the new businesses the contestants are creating.

Shanghai buzz

Back in Shanghai at the diner, Chinese entrepreneur Wang passes his business card to me. It identifies him as Gary Wang, founder, Tudou.com, which translates as "couch potato." Indeed, the site has addictive personalized playlists and mini video sites that he claims can be customized even more with layouts, colors, and music than YouTube. The site features standard stuff: cute kitties, avant-garde clips, and demos of favorite recipes. An overseas returnee, Wang, age 34, exemplifies the tech talent that is transforming China. His résumé is power-packed: grad degrees from Johns Hopkins University and France's INSEAD and management posts at Hughes Electronics Corp. and the German media conglomerate Bertelsmann.

Video sites are a new way for members of China's first me generation to express themselves in the country's newly emerging capitalist economy. "I started Tudou as a way to give power to the people," says Wang, who grew up in southeastern Fuzhou as the son of medical doctors and came to the United States at age 19 on a scholarship to the College of Staten Island. "There was a need for self-expression in China. We allow more room for users to change things than most sites. It is amazing what they can do with a little freedom."

Tudou is one of several struggling but promising video sites that have emerged in China's always-on economy. Not a moneymaker yet, it has $27 million in the bank from venture capitalists.[18] Revenues are insignificant, with video ads by the big brands Adidas, Lenovo, and Sony the major source. Tudou streams 25 million videos daily, not bad compared with YouTube at 100 million. The Chinese video site crashes about once a month from traffic surges. Tudou is likely to be snapped up, but so far there have been no offers such as Google's $1.6 billion purchase price for YouTube in October 2006.

After the video demonstration, Wang suggests that we tour his office. We pass Shanghai's gleaming high-rises in downtown Puxi, cross Suzhou Creek, and arrive at a gritty district called Warehouse Creativity Park that is home to dozens of young companies. The place reminds me of San Francisco's shabby South of Mission area, the once-hip home of Internet start-ups, including the new economy magazine *Red Herring*, where I was an editor at the height of the dot-com bubble.

In a page out of Google's manual, Tudou's small staff of 43 has stock options and gets free meals delivered daily; this is a time-saver since there are no restaurants near Tudou's new headquarters. It's in a hard-to-find warehouse that once stored fruit, about a 20-minute walk from Shanghai's public plaza, People's Park.

Wang's tall lean frame leads the way as we bound up three flights of stairs, turn the corner, and open the door to a funky loft to find a dozen software designers staring at computer screens. Never mind the huge white stuffed gorilla lounging on the faux staircase or the colorful graffiti splashed all over the walls, the result of a manic party to celebrate the office opening. The loft is well equipped for 24/7 work and sports an exercise bicycle, a treadmill, and a pup tent for the occasional overnighter. It's a scene straight out of the late 1990s dot-com era in the United States. Only the flashing neon lights of Shanghai's futuristic skyscrapers on the other bank prove we're not in Silicon Valley.

 part one

THE COPYCATS

CHAPTER ONE

In a remarkable feat of reverse engineering and sheer chutzpah, the Chinese-born and westernized entrepreneur Robin Li took what he learned in Silicon Valley to beat Google in China by inventing a superior search engine in Mandarin. Less than a decade later, he became a multimillionaire and tech superstar in his homeland.

Baidu—
China's Boldest Internet
Start-Up

In the sprawling metropolis of Beijing, it takes an hour to go from the Forbidden City, China's centuries-old Imperial Palace, to a modern high-technology zone some 10 miles to the northeast. On Chang'an Boulevard, which cuts east-west through the heart of Beijing, my taxi crosses several ring roads or expressways that circle the capital while dodging pedestrians and crowded buses spewing fumes as we crawl at a speed typical of a Los Angeles freeway during rush hour. Horns are a constant blare, and I find myself feeling nostalgic for the bicycles that just five years ago filled this wide boulevard. Watching the chaotic scene from the backseat of one of the city's dusty red cabs, I have the windows up and the air-conditioning on full blast to shut out the noise and the choking yellowish pollution.

Finally, we arrive at my destination: the Zhongguancun high-tech district for Internet and software start-ups. Bordering the northern route of the Fourth Ring Road are one high-rise headquarters after another, just as

Yahoo!, Oracle, Cisco, and Intel border Highway 101 in Silicon Valley, from the San Francisco airport to San Jose. The taxi driver pulls into the entranceway of a corporate tower whose peculiar-sounding name—Ideal International Plaza—symbolizes the optimistic spirit of China's new entrepreneurial era. Another sign of the country's rapid economic progress is an automobile showroom on the ground floor. Here the new China beckons, with late-model BMWs on display that could turn heads in Beverly Hills.

Upstairs, on the twelfth floor, is the headquarters of an icon of China's emerging tech economy: the country's leading search engine—not Google but Baidu (pronounced "Buy-Do"). I'm here to interview Robin Li, the firm's founder and CEO and one of China's most famous and successful Internet entrepreneurs. Li does not have the instant name recognition of Larry Page or Sergey Brin, the computer nerds who invented Google while studying at Stanford. But in China, Li is a tech superstar, idolized by hordes of wannabe entrepreneurs.

Li is the mastermind behind China's biggest and arguably best search engine, his first start-up. He is a pioneer among China's young tech founders, the sea turtles who largely copied American dot-coms, adapted them by giving them localized features, and made a fortune.

Li owes his stardom to a melding of the Silicon Valley and Chinese cultures. He cranked up Baidu in Beijing in 1999, raised funds from venture capitalists in the Valley, and borrowed an idea that made the Bay Area an entrepreneurial hot spot: stock options for new staffers, most of whom were young Chinese engineers new to capitalism and entrepreneurship.

Li imitated three high-flying U.S. tech companies before powering up his final and winning strategy. Like Google in the United States, Baidu became the go-to place in China for tips on restaurants and answers to questions about everything from health to physics.

Li then out-Googled even the innovative Google in China. His little search engine that could didn't have the resources of the Google machine but was able to push uphill. Baidu has a speedier and more reliable search engine that produces more precise searches in the Chinese language Mandarin. It also offers more localized features, such as instant messaging, a hit with Chinese Internet users. The home-court advantage and cloning strategy made Baidu a moneymaker in 2004.

The next year, at record speed even for the fast-paced Chinese Internet economy, investment bankers from Goldman Sachs in Asia and Credit Suisse

First Boston began lobbying for Baidu to go public on the Nasdaq stock exchange. Several other Chinese firms were listed on Nasdaq by that time, including the digital advertising firm Focus Media and the online gaming players Shanda Interactive and Tom Online.

On August 5, 2005, Li rang the opening bell to mark the public listing of his five-year-old start-up. A novice entrepreneur born in a poor inland city in China, he was understandably thrilled—and overwhelmed. He stared in disbelief as Baidu's share price zoomed from $27 to $122: the best performance on Nasdaq since the dot-com boom's peak in 2000.

Baidu ended the year with market capitalization of $288 million, outranked only by 5 of the 26 Chinese companies then trading on the exchange. Unlike many highfliers that later crashed, Baidu's shares have nudged up steadily, even passing $400 by November 2007. The awe-inspiring initial public offering and Li's substantial stake in Baidu made him an instant multimillionaire, though not in the same league as Page and Brin. Li is the twenty-sixth richest person in China, with a net worth of $645 million, according to the Forbes 400 Chinese ranking in 2006.

Today, not only do women cast admiring glances at the boyishly handsome 39-year-old, but Chinese youngsters are growing up wanting to walk in his footsteps. He has proved that tech entrepreneurship—a booming area of China's modern economy—is a road to riches. "Robin is a confident, thoughtful Chinese visionary who leads his team with grace," says Tim Draper, founder and managing director of the Silicon Valley venture firm Draper Fisher Jurvetson. "I would not be surprised if Robin built Baidu to be the most valuable company in the world." Draper is not timid about using hyperbole, particularly when it involves Baidu, a company his firm funded.

But whether Baidu can sustain its market lead over a newly reinforced Google in China is debatable. The company has benefited from an insider's advantage and a head start in the market. It's also been criticized for questionable practices, among them establishing links to pirated music files and downplaying search results for companies that stop advertising on its site. Moreover, some recent tests comparing Baidu with an improved local Google search engine have given Google the nod for better results, says the Beijing tech consultant Mark Natkin of Marbridge Consulting Group. "Google is a really clever company, and they have technology that's ahead of the trend," he says.

I can't wait to meet Li and find out what he has that Google's best and brightest haven't been able to beat. At Baidu's headquarters in Beijing, the elevator rises swiftly. The doors open to a bland space filled with rows of cubicles. Baidu could take a lesson from Google's cool-looking campus in Mountain View. I'm shown into a conference room with a distant view of Beijing University, where Li graduated in 1991 with a degree in information management. In strides Li, trimmer and shorter than I imagined. Walking purposefully across the room, he shakes my hand and introduces himself softly: "Hi, I'm Robin Li." He says it humbly, with no trace of the arrogance commonly found among the Larry Ellisons of the United States.

I'm surprised by how reserved he is. An entrepreneurial antihero who has been schooled in the "show no chrome" Chinese culture, Li acknowledges that his success has far outstripped his wildest fantasies. "My dream was to make a technology or product that would be used by as many people as possible. I never thought I would be managing a company this size," he says, sounding overwhelmed by the 750-plus employees he now oversees.

"I can't predict how big the market will be in China, but I have no doubt that we will become bigger than Google."

Robin Li,
cofounder, chairman, and CEO, Baidu

Li is convinced that Baidu is poised to surpass its American rival and become the world's biggest search engine company within 10 years. "The search engine market in China is still small compared to the developed world. Our revenues are a very small fraction of Google's," he explains. "I can't predict how big the market will be in China, but I have no doubt that we will become bigger than Google," he says emphatically.

In China, Baidu is the leading Web site, far outdistancing the seventh-ranked Google. Globally, Baidu is midget-sized compared to the giant Google. Li's search engine ranks seventh among the top Web sites in the world, right after the powerhouses Yahoo!, MSN, and YouTube.[1] Baidu's revenues will more than double in 2007 but will barely tip the scales at a mere $224 million, up from $107 million in 2006, says the former Piper Jaffray analyst Safa Rashtchy, compared with Google at $12.6 billion for 2007, up from $10.6 billion in 2006.

In China, Baidu is gaining on Google and other rivals as the market consolidates. Baidu's market share climbed to 58 percent in mid-2007, up from 47 percent a year earlier, reports the Beijing-based research outfit Analysys International. Meanwhile, the second-ranked Google moved up from 15 percent in mid-2006 to 21 percent in the first half of 2007.

If someday Baidu towers over Google not just in China but worldwide, it will be due partly to Li's abilities and his ambitious plans to enter overseas markets. He's already gone into the huge Japanese market, and Europe is rumored to be next. But it's also a numbers game. China has a population of 1.3 billion, the world's largest, and a rapidly growing number of Internet users.

Within three years, China's Internet population is projected to surpass that of the United States. There are 185 million American Web users, currently the world's largest market, compared with 162 million in China. By 2010, more than 227 million people in China will have Internet access, and the U.S. number will be 196 million.[2] Today, only about 11 percent of China's people log on to the Web, mostly in big cities where Web-surfing youngsters crowd smoky Internet cafés.

The engine that is driving Baidu's growth is the booming market for online advertising and paid searches in China. Ads on Chinese Web sites will nearly double to $1.5 billion by 2010 from $740 million in 2007, projects the research firm Analysys, and paid searches will double to $500 million in 2007, up from $206 million in 2006; these are still small numbers compared with the United States.[3]

Baidu now faces the biggest threat in its six-year history: a local Google makeover. After fumbling with an initially inferior Chinese search engine launched in 2000, Google has marshaled its considerable resources to take on Baidu. Over the last two years, the American powerhouse has planted roots in China, hired the experienced Kai-Fu Lee from Microsoft as its president, introduced a faster and more reliable search engine run from servers in China, and recruited more engineers to fine-tune Google to run in Mandarin. By doing business on Chinese soil, however, Google has submitted to censorship of its new Chinese search engine. The communist-controlled nation censors all Web sites operating in China.

Li's long march

With Google taking direct aim, Li is fired up. His miraculous rise from shy computer scientist to tech star has its roots in Yangquan, an inland Chinese city of 1.2 million people in a coal-mining area some 380 kilometers southwest of Beijing. The fourth of five siblings, Li Yanhong grew up there during the Cultural Revolution and later became known by his English name, Robin.

Bright enough to get into Beijing University, Li was a sophomore in 1989 when the Tiananmen Square political uprising and shootings led to the brief closing of his college campus. A disheartened Li began looking for new horizons. Undergraduate degree in hand, he applied to study in the United States, landed a fellowship at the State University of New York-Buffalo, and earned a master's degree in computer science in 1994, concentrating on information retrieval: the roots of search.

Li learned about the rewards of entrepreneurship while working for American tech firms. For five years he had software jobs at Dow Jones & Co. and Infoseek, a Disney-owned search company. He was a senior consultant at IDD Enterprises, an online financial data service and the publisher of the weekly *Investment Dealer's Digest*, when Dow Jones acquired IDD in 1995; Li's boss, Larry Rafsky, pocketed several million dollars from the deal. "Before I came to America, my impression was that my chances of being a success were not good. But after seeing his success," says Li, "I saw that with tech entrepreneurship, you can make a great success."

Li began dabbling in a side project that involved developing software for the online edition of *The Wall Street Journal*. Soon, he figured out a computerized method for sorting through vast amounts of information on the Internet by ranking Web sites according to the number of related links. When Dow Jones showed no interest in his search technology, Li left the firm in June 1997 and got a patent in the United States. His former boss Rafsky, who today runs the publishing software firm Acquire Media Corp. in New Jersey, praises Li as "one of the smartest and hardest-working people you will ever meet."

At the same time that Google cofounders Page and Brin were tinkering with mathematical formulas for searching the Web, Li was doing the same thing. In the summer of 1997, as Page and Brin hit upon the ranking formula that later made Google a runaway success, Li demonstrated his technology at a U.S. computer conference. There he met William Chang, the chief technology officer of pioneering Internet search engine Infoseek Corp., and soon signed on as staff engineer.

"William persuaded me to join him, and he wanted me to develop the first-generation search engine," says Li. He recalls spending the first two weeks holed up in a conference room writing software codes during the height of the Internet boom. His hopes were dashed, however, when Walt Disney Co. acquired Infoseek in 1999 and sidelined his project. However, his entrepreneurial instincts kicked into high gear when Li's boss became an instant millionaire from the sale. That was the push Li needed to return to China and start his own business.

"I am Chinese, and I see that the Chinese economy is very strong. I see that China is five years behind the United States with the Internet, and I am not sure how many opportunities there are in the United States," says Li, who found lots of potential in China, just as people did in Silicon Valley in the 1990s. Li was so strongly influenced by the feverish start-up activity in the Valley that he penned a book, *Silicon Valley Business War*, that was published in 1999 by the Beijing-based science and engineering school Qing Hua University; that book chronicled the early dot-com battles among Yahoo!, Netscape, and other Internet leaders.

On my next trip to Beijing in fall 2006, after I had interviewed Li a few months earlier, I seek out sources to clue me in on Baidu's meteoric rise. I observe colleagues in Beijing automatically turning to Baidu as their source for answers to anything.

My quest leads to Li's low-profile cofounder, Eric Xu, whom I've tracked down through Fan Zhang, an early investor in Baidu. On a late Sunday morning, I phone Xu and leave a voice message, explaining the reason for my call. Surprisingly, he returns my call within 15 minutes. We book an appointment to meet in Shanghai the next week.

Secret sauce

I catch up with Xu at the executive lounge of the Intercontinental Hotel in the new Pudong section of Shanghai. During a fascinating two-hour-plus interview, he relates the previously untold early history of Baidu. The journey began in Silicon Valley circa 1997, when Xu and Li were introduced by Li's wife, Melissa, a Ph.D. biology graduate of Rutgers University who knew Xu through the biotech community. Xu and Li became friends, bonding through their Chinese heritage and similar interests. As intellectually gifted as Li, Xu was a Beijing University graduate with a doctorate in biology from Texas A&M University and experience at two U.S. biotech start-ups.

Not only was Xu entrepreneurial, but he was well connected to key investors in the Valley. Xu made those connections in 1998 and 1999 while filming a documentary called *A Journey to Silicon Valley*, which later aired on the Chinese national television network CCTV. In some 120 hours of taping, Xu interviewed Valley legends such as John Chambers, chairman and CEO of the tech stalwart Cisco Systems; Albert Yu, the now-retired programmer at Intel Corp.; and venture capitalists Steve Jurvetson of Draper Fisher Jurvetson and Bob King of Peninsula Capital. After watching Xu's documentary at Stanford, Li was energized. He asked Xu to lunch the next day to discuss his brainstorm.

At a Chinese restaurant in Sunnyvale, California, Li pitched Xu to become his partner. "I wasn't sure at first. I had two other start-up projects I was working on," recalls Xu, who is now 43 years old. "If I was able to get funding for either one of them, I was going to quit my job."

But Xu was won over by the persistent Li and his bold idea. Reaching out to his network, Xu persuaded King to hear Li's idea. In less than a week—short even for that heated era—King came on board and lassoed a second investor, Integrity Partners. They anted up a combined $1.2 million in late 1999.

"When Baidu got the money and my two ventures didn't, both Robin and I quit our jobs in mid-December," says Xu, who bagged his other ideas. "We made a commitment to the idea and got on an airplane to Beijing. We found an office space and started hiring employees." Just a few weeks after returning to their homeland, the cofounders opened their shop doors on January 18, 2000, in Beijing.

The serious-minded cofounders named their young firm Baidu, which translates as "seek for truth" and represents a persistent search for the ideal. The name comes from an ancient Song dynasty poem chosen to signify the start-up's Chinese heritage. An English-language investor relations page on Baidu's site attempts to explain the complex, spiritual poem, saying that it "compares the search for a retreating beauty amid chaotic glamour with the search for one's dream while confronted by life's many obstacles."

Sharing the story of Baidu's roundabout path to success, Xu relates how engineers were hired straight out of China's top universities. The new recruits were cheered on with examples from the Valley to persuade them to work hard, grow the company, and get rich. Xu and many of the initial employees did get rich from their stock options in the publicly listed Baidu. Xu became a multimillionaire and today invests in and advises Chinese start-ups.

"We share the overall vision with them. We brainwash them about why Silicon Valley has become so famous," says Xu. "We took the secrets of the Silicon Valley culture: tolerance of failure and tolerance of differences and free flow of information with no barriers. We tell them that we have a democratic environment and that they, as bright engineers, can turn their ideas into products. These are the fundamentals of creating innovation," Xu tells me as we sit in comfortable chairs overlooking a smog-filled skyline. "It was a tremendous start-up experiment. We were not sure we were going to make it."

Indeed, they almost didn't. Xu relates how Baidu failed with three near clones of successful U.S. Internet businesses before finally turning a profit with a fourth plan: a Google-like search engine designed for consumers.

Their first business plan was based on Inktomi, a search engine for portals rather than a stand-alone Web site. "We were going to be a Chinese Inktomi," says Xu, referring to the once high-flying California engine that peaked with a market capitalization of $20 billion during the dot-com boom. "We felt that we could raise money from venture capitalists with this model." And they did: $1.2 million in 1999.

> "It was a tremendous start-up experiment. We were not sure we were going to make it."
>
> **Eric Xu,**
> cofounder, Baidu

Then the Internet bubble began to deflate. Inktomi was snapped up by Yahoo! in 2002 for $200 million, a fraction of its prior value. In China, Li and Xu had little negotiating power over prices and saw many clients gobbled up by larger rivals in the weakening tech economy.

In record time, they came up with a second idea: copy a rapidly expanding Boston-based content delivery network called Akamai Technologies, which routed Web traffic through nearby servers to speed up downloads. Needing cash to keep going, the cofounders hit the fund-raising trail for both the Inktomi and Akamai plans. In September 2000, right before the tech economy meltdown, they landed $10 million.[4]

But by 2001 dot-coms and portals were going bust, and Baidu couldn't collect its payments. With a count of two strikes, Li and Xu tried a third time. They followed yet another Valley company, Verity Inc., which sold search and data management services to large enterprises, but that deal also flopped. "We found that enterprises in China wouldn't pay for specialized search engines," Xu notes. "They wanted the cheapest products, or they went for rip-offs."

Finally, in 2002, with their hopes high and their cash dwindling, Li and Xu took a hint from Google and plunged into the consumer market with a moneymaking model Google had used the year before: paid search from online advertisers.[5]

Paid search, or pay-per-click, works this way: Say a consumer is searching for sneakers and a Nike-sponsored listing pops up on the right-hand side of the Google results. Each time the shopper clicks on a sponsored ad, the search engine company collects a fee from the marketer. The decision to rely on paid search for revenues, as Google was doing, was very risky.

"While Google is now making lots of money from paid search, it wasn't all that clear that the paid search business model would work," Xu recalls. "Robin has a very good strategic vision; he sees things others don't." Today pay-per-click ads account for as much as one-third of all online ad revenues and are the primary revenue stream for consumer search engines.

Li's paid search plan stirred up heated debate at boardroom meetings at Baidu. The Chinese venture capitalist Fan Zhang, then a board member at Baidu and now a managing partner at Sequoia Capital China, recalls the controversy over whether the latest strategy would work. Zhang has invited me to tag along with him on a visit on a fall Saturday afternoon in Beijing at a cool company he's funded, Zhanzuo.com, an alumni networking site that works like Facebook. A Chinese TV film crew is in tow, documenting Zhang's work as though he were a celebrity. Lounging on a red couch cushion in the start-up's hip offices during a film break, Zhang recalls how Li argued his case. "We looked at Google, which was beginning to monetize its business through search, and we looked at the fundamentals of why," he recalls. "We knew that if Baidu shifted the business plan, it would have a dramatic effect on cash flow." Would cash pour in or stop?

Ultimately, Zhang tells me, the board opted to try Li's fourth scheme, in effect becoming the Google of China. Going up against a terrific competitor such as Google was daring enough, but going head to head with prior customers—portals with their own in-house search capabilities—could have been fatal.

The young, inexperienced Baidu team unabashedly borrowed the design of the new Web site from the clean-looking Google home page, using a plain search box with a sparse white background. It designed its colorful red and blue logo with a paw print that some say looks suspiciously like a dog's print. The Chinese word for *dog* sounds like a common mispronunciation of the word *Google* in Chinese. Xu denies any connection. He explains that the cofounders paid a graduate student $400 to design the logo with the imprint of a bear paw. Only a bear's speed, sure-footedness, and endless foraging for food could possibly symbolize Baidu.

There was nitty-gritty work to do too, such as convincing advertisers in China that online marketing could work. Baidu set up a national network of advertising resellers in some 200 major Chinese cities to educate newly capitalistic businesses about the power of online advertising, a basic step Google had bypassed in the far more developed U.S. ad market. It worked. In 2004, two years after the last overhaul, Baidu began making money.

Not taking chances, the cofounders returned to the money well the same year. This time they raised $15 million from DFJ ePlanet and a surprise investor, Google, which put up $5 million and took a 2.6 percent stake. Google was getting trounced by Baidu and was looking to partner with or acquire its Chinese rival. By July 2005, it appeared that a deal-making match was in the works when Google's chairman and CEO, Eric Schmidt, visited Baidu. But that talk was squelched a month later, in August 2005, when Baidu went public on Nasdaq.

DFJ ePlanet, Baidu's largest backer, made a 33 percent return on its 28 percent investment stake, according to chairman and CEO, Asad Jamal, a former board director. Jamal points out Baidu is his firm's "best deal and best exit" of 27 deals, 13 of them in Asia. "Baidu had a fundamental innovation in technology, which was a prerequisite. It had a search algorithm that is more relevant in Mandarin," he explains.

But Google was not about to surrender. The battle peaked in the summer of 2005, when Google set up an office in China and appointed Kai-Fu Lee as its president. The high-profile hiring of Lee, a former Microsoft vice president and head of the software giant's research division in China and Asia, set off a legal battle between Microsoft and Google over a noncompete clause in Lee's contract. That dispute was settled by an agreement that the seasoned manager could have a hands-on role in research at Google only after a one-year hiatus.

> *"Baidu had a fundamental innovation in technology, which was a prerequisite. It had a search algorithm that is more relevant in Mandarin."*
>
> **Asad Jamal,**
> chairman and CEO, ePlanet Ventures

In January 2006, Google CEO Schmidt traveled from Silicon Valley to Beijing to put the company's muscle behind Google.cn (the *cn* stands for "China"). This was a Mandarin-language search engine run from China, not from California. Officially named *Gu Gee* and pronounced "goo-guh," the overhauled Google.cn translated as "harvesting" and had better search capabilities in Mandarin. Searches were speedier and more reliable with servers inside China, and engineers were hired by the dozen to figure out how to make Google outperform Baidu in China. In June 2006, Google sold its shares in Baidu for more than $60 million, a nice return on its earlier $5 million investment.

But to set up business on Chinese soil, Google's top management in the United States had to agree to Chinese government censorship. That put Google.cn on an equal footing with Baidu, which had been censored from the start. Google had to wipe out politically sensitive and banned topics, going directly against the Internet's ideal of free expression and Google's principles of "do no evil." Topics such as the 1989 student uprising at Tiananmen Square don't appear on Web pages in China.

Censorship of Internet sites in China is a hot political topic. Yahoo! has come under fire on Capitol Hill for handing over the names of two bloggers. One was sentenced to prison for eight years in 2003 for criticizing official corruption, and the other was jailed in 2005 for 10 years for blasting human rights abuses in China.

While agreeing to censorship, Google has built in some safeguards to protect users' privacy. Google.cn comes without any blogging or e-mail services. Without access to the names of individual users, Google isn't forced to turn over identities to Chinese officials. By contrast, Baidu offers both blogs and e-mail.

Google provides Chinese users two options besides the censored site: the original, uncensored Chinese-language search engine run from California, although with unreliable service and occasional blocks, and the standard English-language www.google.com that is available worldwide. My searches on the English site in China have been quirky, however. Queries about innocuous business topics occasionally have turned up blank screens. A couple of times, my searches were redirected mysteriously to Baidu.

Google's China plan

In October 2006, I hear Google's side of the story from Kai-Fu Lee. Google's towering new headquarters in Tsinghua Software Park are hard to miss. Entering the lobby during a warm afternoon, I admire a giant Google Earth digital map of the area. The Google map service exists in China as an online Yellow Pages directory, but a rollout is planned soon for mobile phones. I can't help noticing Google's strategic location between Beijing University and Tsinghua University. Here it can tap the top engineering graduate students, and it does.

I'm escorted into a white-walled, sparsely decorated conference room. Google is not giving away any trade secrets here. Now that Google has operations in China, Lee tells me he's confident Google will catch up. He outlines a step-by-step strategy. "First, build a world-class team, use that team working with rest of our world R&D teams to build a world-class product, use the quality of the product to win traffic, and then, with that traffic, will come revenue," he says. "That's how we've done it in the United States, that's how we did it in Europe, and that's how we're going to do it in China."

Lee says that Chinese search users instantly gravitate to the new site once they recognize that it is clearly better. "We have a competitive product now, and we are certain we will have a superior product in the very near future," he says.

Google has hired 100 engineers in China—more than in all the rest of Asia—to improve its Mandarin-language search capabilities. One challenge is finding easier ways for users to input Pinyin or Roman letters that signify sounds in Mandarin. Another task Google has linguists working on is better delineating words in Chinese characters that don't clearly define white spaces. "We hire the top tier of the top tier, and we can be sure that 100 percent of our offers will be accepted on campus," Lee says.

Lee tells me that Google's global reach constitutes a huge advantage over Baidu. "Nobody should be content with only being able to read information from one country. Chinese content comprises only 10 percent of the worldwide Internet. I think every Chinese citizen should want to and demand that they have the ability to access content created in the United States, Europe, or anywhere else in the rest of world."

"We have a competitive product now, and we are certain we will have a superior product in the very near future."

Kai-Fu Lee,
president, Google China

What about putting in more interactive community features such as the online chats that Baidu benefits from? "It's debatable if community-building features are relevant to search," he says.

Sniffs Baidu cofounder Xu, "Lee is a tech guru, but he is not a search expert. It's been proved that community features work best with Chinese searches." He adds, "Google has made more misjudgments in China than in the rest of the world." Tangos Chan, publisher of *China Web 2.0 Review* in Beijing, agrees with Xu. "Google China did not think locally," he says.

Indeed, Baidu is ahead of Google with several innovative local features. Post Bar lets users type in a query and land on a message board to chat with peers and get responses. Baidu Knows lets individuals share knowledge and collect virtual points for giving the best answer. Baidu also offers searches over mobile phones to find, for instance, the McDonald's closest to the next subway stop. Baidu began offering mobile search in March 2006, and it took Google nearly a year to catch up. Baidu also offers multimedia searches, including video clips, which Google does not offer yet.

Borderline illegal

One Baidu feature that Google.cn will never have is links to sites where youngsters can type in the names of Chinese pop tunes and then download MP3 digital music files for free, many of them presumably pirated songs. "It's borderline illegal," Lee says with disgust in his voice. "All those downloaded MP3 files are pirated copies." Google instead offers links to music stores.

The highly popular but controversial MP3 searches account for as much as 20 percent of the searches on Baidu, admits cofounder Xu. "This kind of search can't be monetized like paid search can," he says, meaning that there is no advertising support. Facing lawsuits claiming that it violates copyright laws by offering access to online music files, in early 2007 Baidu began to collaborate with several music labels and cable networks on authorized downloads.

Meanwhile, Li remains focused on running a fast-growing public business. Late in 2006, he recruited his former mentor from Infoseek, William Chang, as Baidu's chief scientist. In 2008, he's also launching a consumer e-commerce service, an area outside Baidu's core focus.

Taking Baidu beyond its comfort zone, in late 2006 Li unveiled plans to enter the large Japanese search market, making good on a vow he made to me a few months earlier about launching outside China. The Japanese paid search market is at least $700 million, roughly three times larger than the Chinese market, according to Richard Ji, an Internet research analyst at Morgan Stanley in Hong Kong. He says that a Japanese search engine may help Baidu link small Chinese companies to Japanese consumers and businesses, which may have strong interests in the inexpensive goods made in China.

The Japanese entry pits Baidu against entrenched Internet leaders Yahoo! and Google in that huge and far-costlier market. Nevertheless, Li, who conducted six months of prelaunch research into Japanese-language search technology, is spending $15 million, or 14 percent of Baidu's budget in 2007, on the expansion. "We believe that our proven strength in non-English-language search, the high Internet penetration in Japan, as well as similarities between the Chinese and Japanese languages make this market an ideal next step for Baidu," Li says.

If he pulls it off, Li will be among the first Chinese entrepreneurs to take a domestic Chinese Internet brand and plant it offshore. Could the next step be other Asian countries? Or possibly a search engine for Chinese speakers in America? Or sites in Europe, as already rumored?

At the very least, the story of Baidu and its soft-spoken China-born CEO demonstrates that China is becoming more than a nation of me-too technologies. Yes, it's true that Baidu has the local edge in China and has not had to face the same criticisms as Google over privacy and free speech issues, ideals that Americans hold dear. Moreover, it's fair to say that Google has far more resources focused on the much larger American search market than on the still-tiny Chinese market. Yet even though Google has gone native in China and is putting more oomph into beating Baidu, my bet is that Baidu will continue to one-up Google in China with its homegrown smarts. More significantly, Baidu may be a harbinger of future technological breakthroughs in China.

The next chapter chronicles how a wizard of an entrepreneur, Jack Ma, has cast a spell over China's Internet scene by creating the country's leading e-commerce site, Alibaba, raising a record $1.5 billion in an initial public offering, and absorbing Yahoo! China in a headline-grabbing $1.6 billion deal from Yahoo! CEO Jerry Yang. Ma also one-uppped Meg Whitman with an eBay-crushing online auction site called Taobao. Talk about a Chinese tech entrepreneur with global influence!

CHAPTER TWO

Not even Harry Potter's author could come up with a tale as magical as Jack Ma's. He rose from the ashes of the Cultural Revolution to head China's best known Web business, Alibaba, and created a template for running an American brand offshore. This is the story of a hometown boy who beat the global champions Yahoo! and eBay, with some accusations of dirty tricks mixed in along the way. Ma's biggest milestone came in late 2007, when Alibaba went public.

Alibaba—
The Wizardry of Jack Ma

At a recent Asia Society dinner at the stately Palace Hotel in downtown San Francisco, the keynote speaker, Jack Ma, wowed the crowd. Interviewed by a local television anchor, the stick-thin Chinese entrepreneur spoke in pithy sound bites. He had the politicos, investors, and executives forgetting their petits fours as they listened to his captivating tale of an improbable rise to wealth and power. "I'm like the blind man riding on the back of a blind tiger," said Ma, a former English-language teacher who heads up the Alibaba Group. Alibaba is a Chinese Internet powerhouse bootstrapped by Ma that not too long ago was on the edge of bankruptcy. "Alibaba might as well be known as '1,001 mistakes,'" he added. "But there were three main reasons why we survived: We didn't have any money, we didn't have any technology, and we didn't have a plan," said Ma in fluent English and with an actor's perfect timing.

Ma is one of the few Chinese Internet entrepreneurs who has joined the global tech elite. He regularly speaks alongside business luminaries Jack

Welch, Rupert Murdoch, and Alan Greenspan in Asia, Europe, and the United States. He's played host to former U.S. president Bill Clinton at a China Internet Summit. His business maneuvers one-upped both Yahoo! CEO Jerry Yang and eBay CEO Meg Whitman when he acquired Yahoo! China and stole market leadership from the popular auction site eBay. He also beat Bo Shao, the Harvard MBA and Chinese founder of Eachnet, a knockoff of eBay in China.

Today, Ma runs both the world's largest online business-to-business marketplace and Asia's most popular Internet auction site. Now that Alibaba operates Yahoo! China, he's running 2 of the top 10 sites on the Mainland. He recently took the Alibaba.com portion of the company public, which chalked up 2006 revenues of $184 million, on the Hong Kong stock exchange in early November 2007. The initial public offering (IPO) raised $1.5 billion and shares nearly tripled on the opening day, though tumbled by 17 percent a day after the debut. Analysts predicted a further fall and cautioned that the stock was overvalued, at more than 200 times forecast earnings for 2007.

How well an independent-minded, creative thinker like Ma will fare in dealing with the stringent requirements of running a public company is questionable, points out Jeremy Goldkorn, publisher of the Chinese media site Danwei in Beijing. "With a charismatic big boss like Ma, you worry if they will be able to handle it once they go public."

But in San Francisco, Ma's energy radiated throughout the ballroom before a spellbound audience. He showcased the high-quality tech leadership skills emerging in China today after decades of communist repression. "Tech leadership will shift to China, and Alibaba will become a world-leading company," declared a superconfident Ma.

"With a charismatic big boss like Ma, you worry if they will be able to handle it once they go public."

Jeremy Goldkorn,
publisher, Danwei

"He is a good example of the great ideas and strong management that are emerging today in China," said Yahoo! CEO Jerry Yang, who accompanied Ma at the dinner event and a conference of the high-level Committee of 100 Chinese group the next week at San Francisco's Four Seasons Hotel. "This new generation of Chinese entrepreneurs with a more experienced base did not exist five years ago. China-born entrepreneurs are starting to have global influence."

Ma, who is 43 years old, is an unlikely Web pioneer. In contrast to most Internet entrepreneurs in China today, he's a "tech dummy," which is an advantage if you're designing user-friendly Web sites. "A product should be click and get it. If I can't get it, then it's rubbish," says Ma.

Another difference: He's "100 percent made in China," Ma says. Ma grew up, went to school, taught English, and started his first and subsequent Internet businesses in Hangzhou, a large city on the Yangtze Delta some 180 kilometers southwest of Shanghai. I later visited Hangzhou for a behind-the-scenes tour of Alibaba and a peek into what makes Ma tick.

Ma was born in 1964, right before the Cultural Revolution. When he was a young child, his grandfather was tormented for being bourgeois, and his classmates ridiculed him for his "bad family." He got sucked into the revolutionary fervor and desperately wanted to become a Red Guard and spread Chairman Mao Tse-Tung's ideology but was not accepted. As a teenager, he became disillusioned with communist propaganda stating that China was the best country in the world. Later, when he was a young teacher, his anguish over the 1989 Tiananmen Square uprising and shootings was so severe that he could not get out of bed for two weeks. This dramatic series of experiences made Ma a fierce competitor and an independent thinker. Without them, Alibaba would not exist, and Chinese society would not have advanced so far so quickly.

Today, Alibaba.com is a key driver in China's unparalleled economic growth that is helping millions of China's small businesses connect to one another and to the international community through two trading sites. Alibaba China is the largest online marketplace for domestic Chinese business transactions and has 16 million users.[1] The English-language site, Alibaba International, has 3 million users, mostly global buyers and importers searching for and trading with China's numerous suppliers.[2] Click on the Alibaba.com site in the United States, and you get access to an online flea market of more than 35 product categories, in English, ranging from computers to blankets. This site also has links to businesses organized into five geographic markets, including the United States, India, and the United Kingdom. Well-marked sections feature easy-to-find buttons that link users to buyers, sellers, suppliers, trade shows, and seminars.

Ma also runs Chinese consumer auction site Taoboa.com, modeled after eBay; Alibaba College, which is dedicated to molding tomorrow's generation of entrepreneurs; AliPay, an escrowlike online payment service that works similarly to PayPal; and Alisoft, a new online business management software for small companies in China. In August 2007 it added Alimama, an online advertising platform roughly equivalent to Google's AdSense ad slot program, to its lineup.

Alibaba's treasures are not all copycat ideas. Ma introduced AliPay a year before eBay rolled out PayPal accounts in China. He also launched instant messaging so that buyers and sellers could get chummy in striking a deal—a hit in the community-centric online Chinese Web. eBay later borrowed that idea. This is among the first made-in-China Web features to travel beyond the country's borders.

Ask eBay's Whitman or Yahoo!'s Yang about what a fierce competitor he is. Ma says he relies on kung fu-like powers of mental concentration and some $107 million from big-name investors[3] to upstage both of those tech titans in his homeland. "When you are small, you use your brain as your strength," he says.

A trip to Hangzhou

After seeing Ma cast his spell at the San Francisco gatherings, I decided to visit the Web wizard on his home turf. On my next trip to China a few months later, I made a side trip from Shanghai to Alibaba headquarters in Hangzhou. At 6:30 a.m. a car with a driver picked me up at the Shangri-La Hotel in Shanghai and took me on a day-long visit to Alibaba. We drove for about two hours, and the whole way, through the skyscrapers, factories, and open land, the thick smog was always there, making me think of nuclear winter.

Arriving at the city streets of Hangzhou, we made a few U-turns before the driver dropped me off at Chuangye Mansion, East Software Park. At this six-story modern office building, Alibaba houses 2,000 of its 3,000 employees. The lobby shows video displays featuring inspirational clips from Ma. On the upper floors there are a few dot-com relics: a Ping-Pong table and an orange couch. But there's not much lounging here. Workers busily monitor computer trades and handle customer service queries in 10 rows, each row 6 cubicles long.

The tour ends at Ma's office, which hosts a fish tank next to the couch where I'm sitting. He shows up and plops down next to me, hugging a pillow and complaining of jet lag.

During our hourlong interview, I hear about the event that changed his life. As a young boy, Ma biked 40 minutes every day to the Shangri-La Hotel near Hangzhou's scenic West Lake to show foreign tourists around and practice his English skills. There, he met an Australian family who invited him to spend a summer month with them. "Before I went, I was educated that China was the richest, happiest country in the world. But I realized that everything was different from what I was told. Since then, I started to think differently. I didn't follow people but developed my own way of thinking."

His older brother and sister did not fight back when classmates ridiculed them, but Ma says that he did. He also points out that he is still the only family member who can speak English. His mother was a garment factory worker, and his father slaved in a photography shop before becoming the appointed head of a local dramatic arts association. Most evenings, his father had actor friends over. That must have been where Ma picked up his acting skills.

A poor student who flunked two university entrance exams, Ma finally was accepted in 1984 by "the worst university in town": Hangzhou Teachers College. In school, his natural leadership skills shone. He was head of the student union and chairman of the student federation for the entire city. After graduation in 1988, he kept a promise he had made to the college president to stay five years in his first job as an English teacher at the Hangzhou Electrical Engineering Institute even though he was making only $15 per month and didn't want to teach. When he left, he was turned down for several jobs, including assistant to the general manager of a newly opened Kentucky Fried Chicken.

> *"I was educated that China was the richest, happiest country in the world. But I realized that everything was different from what I was told. Since then, I started to think differently. I didn't follow people but developed my own way of thinking."*
>
> **Jack Ma,**
> chairman and CEO, Alibaba Group

It was a trip to the United States in 1995 that introduced Ma to the Internet. He was an interpreter for a trade delegation and was visiting friends in Seattle. Never having used a computer keyboard before, he pecked out the words *beer* and *China* into Yahoo! When his search surprisingly turned up nothing, he vowed to help China get into the Internet mainstream. "When I told my friends in China that I was going to do something called the Internet, they didn't know what I was talking about," said Ma, whose impishness compares to that of Amazon's Jeff Bezos. Upon his return to Hangzhou, he borrowed $2,000 from relatives, coaxed his wife to be his partner, and set up China Pages in 1995, the same year eBay launched and one year after Yahoo!'s debut. China Pages hosted Web sites for China's numerous small businesses and was one of the first Internet companies in the newly opening Chinese market despite limited bandwidth and hours-long downloads of Web pages.

Two years later, Ma left China Pages after an ill-fated joint venture with a subsidiary of the government-owned phone behemoth China Telecom; the control was put in the subsidiary's hands, and that killed the start-up. "It was like an elephant and an ant," said Ma, who had pocketed the largest sum he had ever seen in his life—$185,000—from the deal. Next, China's Ministry of Foreign Trade and Economic Cooperation came to the rescue and put him in charge of information at its newly opened e-commerce initiative for Chinese businesses, the China International Electronic Commerce Center. That post paid off big-time in 1997 when Ma played host to Yang on a tour of the Great Wall and the Summer Palace.

Acting on his entrepreneurial impulses, in 1999 Ma gathered 18 people at his apartment in Hangzhou and pitched them for two hours on his dream of building an online international trade fair for China's numerous mom-and-pop enterprises, which make everything from shirts to toys. He asked each one to commit and put his or her money on the table—all $60,000 of it. In December 1999, as dozens of Internet start-ups debuted in China, Ma started Alibaba.com with global ambitions. He chose the Arabian Nights–inspired name because it means the same thing to people all over the world: "Open sesame" is the command used by the fictional character Ali Baba to enter his cave full of treasures.

One-upping Meg Whitman

But Ma was not content with the successful Alibaba e-commerce site for businesses. His dream was to launch an online auction site for consumers like eBay and to run a news, search, and entertainment site in China like Yahoo! He did both and then some.

In 2003, he took on eBay in China by launching a homegrown Chinese auction site called Taobao ("hidden treasure") that allowed consumers to buy and sell mobile phone charge cards, online game merchandise, and jewelry, among other items. In 2005, Taobao's market share jumped to 59 percent; it then reached a commanding 83 percent by August 2007, counting 30 million users and $2.2 billion in transactions. Alibaba claimed victory over the once-dominant eBay China with richer graphics on its Web site and aggressive marketing tactics such as giving sellers free listing of their goods but charging $250 and upward for extra services such as personalized Web pages. It also scored with locals by using an escrow system in which buyers could return items to sellers even six weeks after the sale, according to the Beijing tech consultant Natkin. "You can't localize a product just by doing a translation," he says.

Rumors have swirled that Ma jumped ahead of eBay through corrupt practices. One of my sources ticked off a list of tricks Ma employed: falsely inflating Web traffic numbers, hiring hackers to disrupt the eBay site, and cozying up with journalists and even taking them to whorehouses in a misguided effort to get good press.

"I have been criticized, but it's not important to me. When you make bold decisions, 70 percent of the people hate you and 30 percent love you," says Ma.

eBay China's troubles began shortly after it acquired an eBay clone called Eachnet for $180 million in 2003 and escalated after the Chinese subsidiary lost its CEO, Bo Shao, in 2004.[4] The Chinese "returnee" Shao had formed Shanghai-based Eachnet in 1999. He told me that he copied the eBay model and jiggered it for China after doing some research on the auction site business in the late 1990s at Boston Consulting Group. After the acquisition, eBay hired a foreigner who did not speak Chinese to oversee the site. The operations were moved to California. Decision making slowed to a crawl, and transmission speeds stalled. It could take nine months to change one line of text on the site.

Then eBay China lost Shao's firm hand at the controls. His wife insisted that they leave Shanghai after her father died from a heart attack, which she blamed on a slow-moving ambulance. The couple shuttled between Silicon Valley's wealthy Atherton community and southern France, making Shao an absentee chairman and further contributing to eBay China's problems. Today Shao heads up two new start-ups in China[5] and is scouting for deals for the U.S. venture firm Matrix Partners.

Scrambling to replace Shao, Whitman installed Martin Wu, a former marketing officer for Microsoft's Greater China region, as CEO in September 2005. She called China the largest e-commerce opportunity in the world and poured $100 million into eBay China in 2005. However, within one year Wu was out, and a few months later, in late 2006, the site was shut down. Vowing not to give up, Whitman formed a joint venture with the billionaire Li Ka-shing's Chinese portal Tom Online, a partner to eBay-owned Skype in China led by Tom Online's CEO, Wang Lei Lei. The partners were planning to launch a new site in the fall of 2007. "We are committed to the Chinese market and remain excited about the future," Whitman said, noting that the new partner will help eBay leverage its "extensive local market knowledge and keen understanding of the lifestyle aspirations of Chinese consumers."

Ma's Yahoo! deal

As Ma's next act after stealing the market lead from eBay China, he lassoed Yang on a windy spring day at the Pebble Beach golf course, where they were attending a Chinese tech outing. During a walk along the beach, Ma told Yang of his dream of running Yahoo! China and merging Yahoo! search into his e-commerce marketplace. He coaxed Yang into letting Alibaba manage his faltering Yahoo! China business, which suffered from lack of local content. In August 2005, in a complex deal that kept Debevoise & Plimpton and other top law firms busy for months, Yahoo! paid $1 billion for a 40 percent stake in Alibaba, and Ma's firm took over management of Yahoo! China.[6] The landmark deal has created a new management template, with Yahoo! effectively outsourcing its business in China to the local player Alibaba, pointed out Morgan Stanley analyst Richard Ji.

Yang didn't have much choice. Yahoo! China has been through several reincarnations and in just the last two years has been first a stripped-down search site and then a portal. "There's a reason Yahoo! China has not been successful for nine years, and to turn it around will take at least three years. It is not a machine but three hundred people," says Ma, who complains that his hair is turning gray from the busiest period in his career. Two years after the acquisition, he is spending three-quarters of his time in Beijing, staying in a hotel near Yahoo! China to work on the turnaround. "I respect Yang for giving their own child to us. It is a big change for them, but they know we can do a much better job."

Local operation of Yahoo! China does raise sensitive issues, however. Because the portal now is run within Chinese borders, it is censored by Chinese government authorities, as all sites are. Yahoo! recently has been criticized for turning over the names of two Chinese bloggers earlier in this decade who were jailed.

But Ma is not concerned about censorship. "We are a business. We're in the Net to improve and change people's lives. We are not into politics," he says. Would he turn over names of Internet users to officials? "I would cooperate if there were criminal charges like terrorism or drugs," he says.

A makeover of the Yahoo! China site was under way in May 2007 when I met its president, Zeng Ming, in Beijing for a rare interview. Zeng, a former professor of management strategy from Cheung Kong Graduate School of Business in Beijing, joined Yahoo! China in August 2006 as vice president of strategy and was named president four months later. He is the third president of Yahoo! China since Alibaba took over. His predecessor, Xie Wen, was in the job only 40 days before he resigned over disagreements about the radical changes needed to fix the portal.

At Zeng's office in a high-rise tower optimistically called the Winterless Centre, he let me in on the new master plan for upgrading Yahoo! China. It involves meshing Yahoo!'s search technology, user-generated content, and a new Web 2.0 portal that includes social networking media into a moneymaking platform set. The new, improved Yahoo! China was set to debut in late 2007. Also in the works is a longer-range plan to integrate Yahoo! search into Alibaba and Taobao. That would put Alibaba at the forefront of a trend toward integrating search with e-commerce so that buyers and sellers can search and find exactly what they want on the first try, a feature eBay also has.

"The Net is about culture. You can't have expats working on it."

Zeng Ming,
president, Yahoo! China

"When we took over Yahoo! China, we knew the transaction would not be easy. Major innovation takes time," says Zeng. The first 12 months were eaten up by integrating teams and processes and recruiting several high-level executives who specialized in search, marketing, and community services. "The big growth will come next year," he promises, ticking off online advertising, paid search, and integrated e-commerce services as key revenue streams.

As part of the remake, much of Yahoo! China's inner workings, including servers and platforms for search and e-mail, are being moved to China too. "The Net is about culture. You can't have expats working on it if you are going to succeed," says Zeng.

He goes on to list another reason why Yahoo! China has a leg up simply because it is run by Chinese in China. "The Net is also about speed. International management slows down procedures," says Zeng.

Alibaba's curse

Just six years ago, Alibaba.com was saved from bankruptcy during the dot-com crash by a nail-biting restructuring after overexpanding during the Internet bubble. The turnaround was orchestrated by newly appointed chief operating officer Savio Kwan, a former General Electric top executive in China. When Kwan was recruited in January 2001, Alibaba had been burning through $2 million per month and had less than $10 million in the bank, recalls Tina Ju, a Chinese venture capitalist and four-time investor in Alibaba. "I saw the sentiment change at the company from Jack Ma's vision of conquering the world in B2B [business-to-business e-commerce] to nearly going bankrupt," she tells me over coffee one morning in the Marriott Hotel lobby in Shanghai. "It couldn't have been done without the visionary and spiritual leadership of Jack Ma," Ju says. "Everyone in Alibaba believed in him."

But it was Kwan who was assigned the painstaking task of pruning the staff. "Jack could have made the job cuts, but it would have been difficult for him to lay off those he had recruited," she explains, adding that the layoffs were "very brutal but necessary."

Kwan cut the high-cost engineering team in the United States from 40 people to 3 in one day. He cut the senior-level marketing team to 10 people; got rid of dozens of highly paid expatriate staff members in Beijing, Hong Kong, and Shanghai; and ended expensive leases. The remaining staffers were given the option of having their salaries cut in half but tripling their options in the company, a process that identified staff members who were true believers in the long-term vision.

Alibaba cut the burn rate (the monthly operating expenses above incoming cash) by 75 percent in just one quarter. The board was impressed, but what next? Alibaba was still using up $500,000 per month and at that rate had 18 months to live.

During board meetings, the investor Ju recalls, presentations were very informative and transparent. "Very few companies do that in China, but here they tell us the worst-case scenario: Here's what we will do if we can't survive; this is what we will do; this is what we will liquidate. We realized they had done everything they possibly could. And the board became extremely supportive even though they didn't know what the answer was," recalls Ju, who served on the board's audit finance committee.

To come out of the depths, the goal was to focus on generating revenues. As a start, Kwan spent three days talking to management about building the company culture, finding the right business model, and building the best sales force. Five or six business areas were identified, with the number one objective being to avoid getting into a business in which bribery was rampant. That eliminated most of the ideas Alibaba was considering, says Ju. Finally, with the goal of generating sustainable revenues and cash flow, Alibaba established an offline catalog of Chinese suppliers with goods to trade, backing off its original online strategy.

In a follow-up mobile phone call with Kwan, he filled me in on more details of the turnaround. Relying on his GE training, Kwan established a management development program in April 2001 to weed out nonperformers and reward the best sales producers. Staffers in the lowest 10 percent of the pyramid were axed. The rest were categorized as rabbits, those who do whatever someone tells them to do; wild dogs, individualists who can perform; or bulls, those who succeed through hard work. Only the bulls were kept.

Kwan also formed a Million Dollar Club for top performers. The membership requirement was RMB 1 million ($132,000). When the first salesperson hit the target, he or she won a prize. Since money was tight, the prize was a poem written by Kwan. The poem idea took off and became part of Alibaba's culture.

The rewards system worked. By 2002, the team had met its goal of eking out a tiny $1 in profits. However, the managers deferred taking a bonus they were supposed to get because revenues missed the mark at only $3.7 million for 2002. But revenues climbed to $30 million in 2003 and then reached $67 million in 2004 and $125 million in 2005, according to Kwan. Today the master plan has hatched an expansive e-commerce business, auction site, and portal with revenues exceeding $200 million.

"The headquarters in Hangzhou outside the central cities of Beijing and Shanghai gave us a chance to put our heads down with minimum interference and minimum interruption," says Kwan. Then in his early to middle fifties, Kwan says he stayed in a $17-a-night hotel for four years to stage the turnaround. Today, Kwan has been pulled out of retirement to help Ma integrate Yahoo! China into Alibaba as "chief people officer" and "chief education officer."

But there is a lot of work to do. Online commerce in China is growing fast but is still tiny. China's e-commerce market was worth $6.5 billion in 2007,[7] nearly a sixfold increase over 2004. Business-to-business e-commerce is the fastest-growing segment, but only about 3 percent of China's 42 million small and medium-sized companies—which make up the vast majority of businesses in the Middle Kingdom—made deals over the Internet in 2006.[8] In the United States, by comparison, nearly all businesses use the Internet to purchase some materials and services.[9]

Only about 15 percent of the Chinese population made a purchase online in 2006, according to iResearch, compared with about 66 percent in the United States. Chinese Internet users do not buy more online because of concerns about security, poor customer service, delivery delays, and privacy. Limited use of credit cards is another deterrent.

Ma's next act

After being at the helm of Alibaba for nearly 10 years, Ma is looking to his next act. As with Alibaba, he wants to do something that will have a positive influence on China's development, "not through war, gas, or bloodshed but by wisdom." On his list of possibilities are big ideas such as environmental protection and reforms in education and agriculture. "There are 800 million farmers in China, and there are ways to help them become more productive and solve the hunger problem," Ma says. "I want to change history, do something important in my life, and influence individuals like we have with millions of small businesses on Alibaba. Then they love and respect you because you made their life important."

"I want to change history, do something important in my life, and influence individuals like we have with millions of small businesses on Alibaba."

Jack Ma,
chairman and CEO, Alibaba Group

With that, Ma got up off the couch and picked up a golf club to practice his swing, which looked pretty good thanks to a professional golf coach. Who can blame Ma for showing off?

Next, we shift to a woman entrepreneur who has figured out how to best Jeff Bezos in China with an online bookselling start-up called Dangdang.com. Peggy YuYu is her name, and she is going head to head with Bezos as he unleashes a plan to win back market leadership for his Chinese business, Joyo Amazon.

Peggy YuYu, a cofounder of the Chinese online bookseller Dangdang.com, has shown how to copy and then outsmart Amazon.com in China. She's also created the largest Chinese online retailer. In the process, she's revolutionized the Chinese book market and probably is headed for an initial public offering.

Dangdang.com— The Amazon-Plus of China

China's largest bookstore, the five-story Beijing Book Store, houses some 230,000 titles and makes a Wal-Mart look small. On row after row of shelves, there are investment books, kids' books, art books, and miles of textbooks. There are best sellers by John Grisham and Stephen King in Mandarin, along with Jack Welch's *Winning* and *The Warren Buffett Way*. On the lower level, I find a small English-language section complete with Dan Brown's *The Da Vinci Code*.

Although the familiar titles make me feel at home, the state-owned store falls short on customer service, convenience, and selection. The aisles are narrow, and the crowds are thick, with students sitting cross-legged on the floor, poring over books. Security guards hover at the escalators. Where's a comfy chair to lounge in and read a book? Where's the coffee shop to pick up a cappuccino and a pastry?

On a second sweep of the frenetic store, I fully grasp how far removed I am from Borders and Barnes & Noble. Although the store is overloaded, appearances are deceptive. Textbooks and English-language instruction books account for half the volumes.

China is opening up to books and their power to educate young and old alike and thus transform society, but shopping for books can be a chaotic and tiresome experience. After another half hour of bumping into people and jostling past cashier lines, I head outside into the glaring noonday sun to catch my breath.

My brief tour shows why buying books online is catching on in the world's fastest-growing book market. Although China invented movable type hundreds of years ago, the Chinese looked to Seattle for a more modern innovation in publishing: online sales. In the northwestern reaches of the United States, the American entrepreneur Jeff Bezos popularized bookselling over the Internet with a start-up called Amazon.com. From its humble beginnings in 1994 as a small online book retailer run from a garage, Amazon.com grew into a $10.7 billion empire.

The Chinese were quick to copy Amazon.com. In 1999, five years after Amazon's founding, dozens of knockoffs sprang up in China. That was also the year Bezos was named Man of the Year by *Time* magazine for making e-commerce the convenient way to shop for books and other merchandise.

But in China Bezos has flubbed his chance to be the king of online book-selling, at least so far. Even though China is Amazon's fastest-growing market, with almost half of its overall revenues coming from international sales, the number one online bookseller in China is a Beijing-based online company called Dangdang.com. Dangdang has nearly 13 million registered users or customers on its site, trailed closely by onetime market leader Amazon's Joyo at 11 million. On a recent trip to China, Bezos declared that Amazon will increase its investment in Joyo and make it "the very best in the world at serving customers."

"The winner will be the one who lasts longer."

Tangos Chan,
publisher, *China Web 2.0 Review*

Which company will emerge as the clear winner in the long term is debatable. The rivals have been jockeying for market leadership for several years. Neither one is currently profitable.

Tangos Chan of *China Web 2.0 Review* places his bet on Joyo because its Amazon parentage gives it access to a large pool of money, an advantage over Dangdang, which is dependent on raising venture capital on favorable financial terms. "The winner will be the one who lasts longer," he concludes.

The pitched battle between the two contenders has set up an interesting contest between domestic and foreign-operated players. Chinese start-ups with overseas parents typically are not as flexible or adaptable to market needs as are locally owned firms, observes Beijing consultant Mark Natkin. "Overseas owners tend to bring over what worked well in the United States or Europe without really considering the local market needs," he says. "On the flip side, deep-pocketed multinational parent companies can leverage company resources and bring more capital and technology to the competition."

> *"My inspiration was to run the largest online retailer in China and to bring a lot of products to consumers."*
>
> **Peggy YuYu,**
> cofounder and copresident, Dangdang.com

Behind Dangdang's success story is a woman who is as genteel as Bezos is brash: Peggy YuYu. Don't be fooled by her personable style, silky voice, and ballerina-like grace or even her easy laugh that is far from Bezos's loud guffaw. She is raw ambition and energetic drive personified. "My inspiration was to run the largest online retailer in China and to bring a lot of products to consumers," she says.

YuYu may not have the star power of the publishing magnate Katharine Graham, but she wants to be in that league. "When I get to the age of Katharine Graham when she wrote about the *Post* and her work, I may decide to write a book myself. Hopefully, by then I will have more interesting things to say," she wrote in an e-mail to me.

It was fate and love that first led YuYu down the Dangdang path in 1999. Working on Wall Street after earning an MBA from New York University, she met a Chinese book publisher who was on a business trip in Manhattan. She soon began going to China to see him. Their love story ended in marriage. YuYu left behind her career and lifestyle in New York City to settle in China in 1998. Back home, she was appalled by the state of Chinese retail outlets, most of them poorly lit, stuffy, and unorganized.

Life in New York City for nearly a decade had shown her that shopping can be fun, with relaxing Saturday afternoons spent browsing neat bookstores in midtown and sleek fashion boutiques on Madison Avenue. Grasping the opportunity to bring a small piece of the consumer culture she had experienced in the West to China, she and her husband, Li Guoqing, set out to revolutionize the Chinese book distribution business. They vowed to make the Internet a key way to sell books in China, just as Amazon.com had done in the United States.

"I saw the sharp contrast in consumerism between the United States and China. It is two different worlds," says YuYu, age 42, who with her short-cropped black hair and round-rimmed glasses looks like a serious-minded librarian. "In the United States, it's almost to the stage of over-retailing," she adds, ticking off major book marketers such as Barnes & Noble, Doubleday, Waldenbooks, and Borders.

But China has no national distribution network and only limited use of credit cards for online purchases. She succinctly sums up why Dangdang stands out in the Chinese book maze. "We made shopping for a book really easy for consumers. That's what we got right," she says. "We wanted people to come to us when they couldn't find things locally." Chinese consumers did exactly that, lured to Dangdang because it offered the widest selection of books online in a market where availability was an issue. Tossing in 40 percent discounts off list prices didn't hurt in a nation where cheap pirated copies are rampant.

Trying harder

YuYu made her start-up tick by relying on strategic instincts, benchmarking, merchandising flair, financial smarts, and an insider's perspective on the local market. In four short years compared with seven years for Amazon.com in the United States, she took Dangdang.com to profitability—with a $40 million assist from venture capital investors in the United States and China. Another asset was YuYu's ability to capitalize and learn from others' mistakes. When Joyo.com slipped after Amazon bought it, she moved right in and tripled Dangdang's sales in one year.

Granted, tiny Dangdang doesn't come near the colossus Amazon.com and probably never will. Nevertheless, in a vast country with few chain stores and no large catalogers, it is the biggest bookstore with some 200,000 titles for sale on its Web site. And YuYu is well on her way to leaving her imprint on China's historic rise as an economic powerhouse. Dangdang has made books widely available in a country where there's a palpable desire for knowledge and getting ahead, with reading being the most democratic route to riches.

These are no small achievements. The $7.8 billion Chinese book market is growing by $300 million per year[1] but is still small compared with the $25.1 billion U.S. market.[2] Book publishing in China is controlled largely by the state and is highly fragmented. Unlike the huge Beijing Book Store, most of China's 100,000-plus bookshops are tiny, with a limited range of titles and few foreign works. The dominant player, the state-owned Xinhua news agency, has some 14,000 stores and until recently was the only national distributor of books. Only in the last few years have new privately owned retail chains such as Xooyo and Xishu emerged in the bigger cities. Savvy foreign retailers began to tiptoe into the burgeoning market after getting permission to own majority shares in bookselling chains in late 2004 after China's entry into the World Trade Organization. It is rare to find a Western-style bookstore like the Beijing Bookworm, a haunt of the city's large expatriate, English-speaking population.

Online book sales offer new, low-priced competition to traditional bookstores and are booming, with business up by about 100 percent annually in recent years. But they still account for only about 2 percent of the total books sold.[3] Internet usage is becoming a part of daily life in China, and e-commerce bounds ahead by nearly 40 percent a year. In 2007, business-to-consumer e-commerce in China will top $955 million (compared with the current U.S. level of $131 billion),[4] and books are leading the charge in online retailing. Books are the top-selling online item in China, accounting for one-third of all consumer merchandise bought over the Internet.[5]

Dangdang is also China's largest online retailer. About 40 percent of its $48 million in revenues comes from general merchandise ranging from brand-name clothes and linens to cosmetics and toys. The books-plus strategy comes directly

"Someone is going to be the Amazon of China, and it's most likely going to be Dangdang."

David Chao,
cofounder and general partner, DCM

from Amazon.com, which today derives about one-third of its revenues from selling electronics, videos, software, and other merchandise online.

"Someone is going to be the Amazon of China, and it's most likely going to be Dangdang," says David Chao, cofounder and a general partner of the venture firm DCM, which is an investor in Dangdang.com. "Peggy and her team put their heads down, humbled themselves, and focused on the nuts and bolts of the business."

Amazon-busting strategy

In Beijing, I interview YuYu. Her office is in the city's Central Business District, which to Beijing is what midtown Manhattan is to the Big Apple. Dangdang's headquarters reflect the threadbare publishing business, a throwback to the shabby *New Yorker* magazine offices on Madison Avenue. YuYu, dressed casually in beige slacks and a silk floral blouse, comes out to greet me at the reception desk.

As we face each other in worn leather chairs in her office, I flash back to a phone call I had a few weeks earlier with Ruby Lu, a partner at DCM, which is YuYu's main backer. After Lu tracked the start-up for several years, she cornered YuYu at a Chinese New Year reception in January 2006. Lu, one of the few native Chinese females in the clubby male-dominated venture capital world and a former Goldman Sachs vice president, parked herself in YuYu's office and refused to accept no for an answer. She beat hordes of contenders to seal her firm's $15 million investment and joined the board at Dangdang.com in July 2006.

Lu gave me some valuable advice. She told me that I should let YuYu know that I live and work in New York City. I take that approach and also compliment YuYu for being the Chinese female entrepreneur who has figured out how to one-up Amazon's Bezos. It works. Soon we're deep into a long conversation during which she tells me what trade secrets she has used to beat Amazon at its own game.

With nearly perfect English thanks to her undergraduate degree in English literature from the Beijing Foreign Language Institute and a decade in the United States, YuYu is the public voice of the company with foreigners like me. Her husband, a sociology graduate from Beijing University and an equal partner in the start-up, does not make an appearance.

Back in 1999 when Dangdang was beginning, China's long-slumbering book trade was awakening in the aftermath of the Cultural Revolution, during which books were burned and intellectuals were jailed. Meanwhile, in the United States, Amazon, with its new Internet distribution system for books, was on fire.

It was easy for YuYu, whose parents were sent to re-education camps during the Cultural Revolution and who was raised by her grandparents in Sichuan province, to envision a better lifestyle for China. What better road to improvements was there than literature? Her husband, a book publisher in China, was equally frustrated by the stark contrast he saw between the consumer-driven West and the more limited selections in his communist-controlled homeland. He found the state-owned bookstores abysmal and the shelf life of even best sellers very short. "My husband hated the way distribution was handled in stores. Both consumers and publishers were poorly served," she says, pointing to the Internet as the means to modernize China's antiquated bookselling business.

From the start, it was clear that they were dreaming big. The repeated syllable in the company's name means "worthy" in Mandarin. It also vaguely sounds like the sound of a cash register opening and closing.

Laying the cornerstone for Dangdang, YuYu and her husband spent two years developing the first comprehensive nationwide database of 200,000 books in China. It categorized books by specific subject matter instead of using broad headings such as history and geography. For example, YuYu points to the traditional way Chinese retailers put a book on how to find a boyfriend in the same place as a sociology textbook. "They use the library science classification system, so it didn't really cater to consumers," YuYu relates, sipping tea while we meet at her Beijing office. Her system has been "copied by everyone now and is almost like the industry standard," she adds.[6]

In November 1999, the Web site was launched thanks to Dangdang's database, which made it possible to search for specific books online, just in time for the Internet boom. By then, Amazon had been in business for four years and had been listed on Nasdaq since 1997; its founder, Bezos, had become a dot-com celebrity. Seemingly every Chinese entrepreneur was a Bezos wannabe. Within months, Dangdang had some 300 competitors.

Dangdang faced China-specific growing pains. One problem was that Chinese consumers weren't used to using credit cards to pay for goods online.

YuYu tried to promote the concept by offering them a 2 percent discount on online orders, but she admits that, "It really didn't work."

Instead, Dangdang resorted to the old-fashioned but popular Chinese system of money orders purchased at a post office. Dangdang later added a cash-on-delivery service. In return for cash, bicycle couriers came to its distribution centers to pick up parcels and delivered the goods. That system is still in place, and Dangdang also offers online payment through billing systems such as PayPal.

As the Internet era crashed and burned in 2000, dot-coms were failing by the dozen in China and the United States. Even the world's largest e-tailer, Amazon.com, seemed on the verge of collapse. In early 2001, Amazon reported a fiscal loss of $1.4 billion, though it squeaked out a profit by the end of the year by laying off workers, streamlining distribution centers, and cutting unprofitable items.

Biggest takeaways

In China, Dangdang emerged as one of the few survivors. Dangdang did not get trapped by the need to ship bulky or heavy goods that ate into its profit margins. It avoided several bad investments that Amazon.com made in dot-com land: the online pet supply store Pets.com, video and snack delivery service Kozmo.com, and an online furnishing store, Living.com. "We had the benefit of a latecomer's advantage," says YuYu as drivers beep their horns loudly on the Beijing streets below. "By the sheer fact we are a couple of years behind our peers in the West, we really could cherry-pick from a lot of things being tested in an elaborate and expensive way and decide what to do and what not to do."

Another valuable lesson was to limit the number of distribution centers. Amazon built as many as 10 but later found it had to streamline its large logistics operation to reduce costs. Dangdang, by contrast, kept overhead costs low by relying on only one distribution center in Beijing and renting storage space from a bookstore retailer in Shanghai and Guangdong. It also has deals with nearly 50 delivery companies to get distribution in some 170 cities in China.

Most important, Dangdang learned not to get swallowed up by a large American firm, especially one called Amazon.com. In early 2004, it must have been difficult to turn down a takeover offer of $75 million from Amazon.com, but Dangdang's co-founders must be pleased that they did. After Amazon acquired Dangdang's chief rival, Joyo, in August 2004 for $75 million, Joyo lost market share and the market lead. The blame was placed on Amazon headquarters in Seattle, which had restructured management at the

"By the sheer fact we are a couple of years behind our peers in the West, we really could cherry-pick from a lot of things being tested in an elaborate and expensive way and decide what to do and what not to do."

Peggy YuYu,

cofounder and copresident, Dangdang.com

cash-starved firm, cut costs, and integrated its new Chinese subsidiary into the parent company. Within months of the Amazon takeover, Joyo's founder and chairman, Lei Jun, resigned. His exit soon was followed by that of several more Joyo managers, executive vice president Chen Nian, president Lin Shuixing, and vice president Chen Xiaohong.

In the prior executives' place, Amazon hired a new president for Joyo with no book publishing experience: Wang Hanhua, a former Asia Pacific top manager for Motorola and director of research at Gallup Consulting in Beijing. Amazon's choice of an executive with no industry experience to run its Chinese subsidiary echoed mistakes made by other large American multinationals that acquired Chinese firms. The shake-up also drew criticism from former Joyo vice president Liu Jun. He contended that Amazon was repeating the mistakes of eBay and Yahoo!, which had failed in China because their local managers lacked quick response skills for the fast-moving Chinese marketplace.

As Joyo.com was in recovery from the sudden jolt of the Amazon takeover, Dangdang plotted its next move. Again following the lead of Amazon in the United States, which began selling toys and electronics goods in 1999, YuYu started marketing general merchandise on its Web site in 2004 in addition to books. "I knew I enjoyed a good store, a good product, and I thought if I can duplicate that for other consumers, it must have commercial value."

The bold move jump-started the firm's growth. Today, sales of items such as women's blouses, bed linens, and toys account for 40 percent of Dangdang's revenues compared with about 25 percent for the Amazon-owned

Joyo. The busy, colorful orange and turquoise site Dangdang runs is hopping with everything from discounts on a new Harry Potter title to Ikea bath towels and Seiko watches to CDs from local pop sensations.

With few exceptions, she has gotten the merchandising mix right for Dangdang's consumers. YuYu handpicks the items for sale on the Dangdang site, and she has a good eye for design. She notices, for example, the Parisian-made Lancel handbag I'm carrying and compliments me on its unusual eggplant-colored leather. The merchandise on her site is sold almost exclusively within China, with no foreign marketing or promotion. Overseas customers can order goods from the site and have them shipped by a courier service such as DHL. She blends local goods with well-known Western brands such as Oil of Olay for the site's customers, who tend to be middle-income city dwellers. "I would like 40 million Chinese buying from Dangdang. I could have so much power over consumers. I could change the way people dress," says YuYu.

Just as benchmarking and copying competitors have given Dangdang a leading edge in China, the strong financial background of cofounder YuYu has been a big plus. YuYu handles finance and accounting plus legal, human resources, and administration, and her husband works in marketing and technology. They make appointments to meet in the office and try not to discuss business at home, where they are raising a 10-year-old boy.

Finance work comes naturally for YuYu, as it does for Bezos, a former investment banker. At age 22, she was asked to accompany a high-level Chinese trade delegation to 12 U.S. cities in 18 days and serve as a translator and ad hoc bookkeeper for the trip, a task that meant recording every penny spent by the provincial government chiefs. She came to the United States in 1987 as an international graduate student at the University of Oregon but dropped out to pursue a business career. She helped negotiate a joint venture for a Chinese power company near Akron, Ohio, and then became a sales manager at a timber company in Cleveland for a year. With her savings, she earned an MBA in finance from New York University. In the early 1990s, she landed a job on Wall Street. There, she spent the next few years working as a partner in a small New York City investment banking firm, advising corporate clients ranging from Chinese companies to large multinationals such as UPS on leveraged buyouts, mergers and acquisitions, and financial projections.

Her knack for taking on hard-core tasks stems from her parents, who were engineers at a power plant in China. They had encouraged their intellectually inclined daughter to pursue a job in China in the booming area of marine port construction. "A lot of the things I was doing then are on a grander scale than what I do now," she reflects as she recalls countless business trips to visit power plants, distribution centers, and law firms with top corporate officials.

Mistake money

Although it was unprofitable in 2006 because of investments in business development, the firm turned its first profit in the fourth quarter of 2003, only four years after its start. It took Amazon seven years to pass the same profit milestone in 1995, and Joyo remains unprofitable. Dangdang was refueled with $11 million in venture money in 2004[7] and took in another $27 million in July 2006[8] as "mistake money" in case of a financial emergency, says YuYu. The next step in Dangdang's short history could be an initial public offering, possibly timed for the 2008 Beijing summer Olympics.

Just like the Chinese search engine Baidu, which copied Google, and the e-commerce leader Taobao, which copied eBay, Dangdang's story of triumphing over a strong American-owned brand by imitating it is by now a familiar theme. In all three cases, astute local managers with Western know-how and experience gathered from American firms' mistakes were essential.

Sure, Dangdang chose a copycat route to victory. But look to YuYu and her husband to gain more confidence and put more originality into their strategic moves from now on. Bezos will have to move swiftly and boldly and use his inimitable imagination and American firepower to keep his Chinese online bookseller Joyo at the forefront.

In the next chapter, we see what happens when a local Chinese competitor has an undeniable lead in a wide-open new market, in this case the booming Chinese automotive market. The company I profile next, Chinacars.com, is a classic story of copycat success. It is also a case study of one of China's leading up-and-comers on the emerging entrepreneurial scene.

CHAPTER FOUR

Car ownership in China is still exceedingly rare, but the dream is becoming a reality. China is destined to become the world's largest car market, with some 15 million newly middle-class Chinese poised to buy their first vehicles in the next three years. Enter John Zhang, who has modernized the all-American AAA brand down to its name: Chinacars Club (CCC). Next, Zhang has his eye on a Nasdaq listing.

Chinacars.com— Cruisin' with Style

The construction cranes are cranking night and day at the Olympics site in Beijing as the city prepares to host the 2008 summer games. The twig-like track and field stadium known as the Bird's Nest already has taken shape—just one symbol of China's progress.

John Zhang still remembers the day the news broke that Beijing had won the competition to host the Olympics. It was July 13, 2001, a historic date for his country and for him.

That was when Zhang, who was out of work after his high-tech Silicon Valley employer went bankrupt, had a eureka moment. That very day, he decided to get on a plane to Beijing, his hometown, as fast as possible. "I needed to be there. This was a special moment for China," Zhang says.

In Beijing, he was caught up in the excitement. People were out in the streets celebrating. Bars were full. Zhang rented the cigar lounge of the St. Regis Hotel and threw an all-night party for his friends.

The same month, China opened another portal in the Great Wall by entering the World Trade Organization, taking a gigantic leap into the global economy and allowing foreign investors and overseas competition to come in.

Zhang quickly concluded that those events marked the beginning of a Chinese century, with Beijing as the nerve center, as China sloughed off years of communism and liberalized its economy.

Zhang felt he could not sit on the sidelines. He had to jump in and capitalize on the wide-open opportunities unfolding in China. Although he never had run his own business before, Zhang decided his time had come in the newly reforming Chinese economy. But what kind of business? He thought about it, but not for too long. What are the top goods and services that China's long-deprived consumers want now that the market is opening up? He ticked them off: a car, a home, travel and education for the kids—an all-American consumer wish list.

> *"I realized that cars were the most important symbol of private ownership in China."*
>
> **John Zhang,**
> president and CEO, Chinacars

As he traveled around Beijing on streets increasingly jammed by traffic where bikes were fewer and fewer, it was a no-brainer. It had to be cars. "I realized that cars were the most important symbol of private ownership in China and would be the strongest engine of growth in the economy," Zhang says. Striking a patriotic theme, he adds: "We carried a sense of history, a sense of country. This was not just a simple business but a part of our lifestyle."

> *"We carried a sense of history, a sense of country. This was not just a simple business, but a part of our lifestyle."*
>
> **John Zhang,**
> president and CEO, Chinacars

Just four months later, on November 15, 2001, Zhang formed Chinacars Inc., an automotive service site for first-time car buyers that so far has avoided major road bumps. Chinacars is a tech-savvy, full-service Chinese version of the American Automobile Association (AAA), that longtime cultural icon founded in Chicago in 1902. Its Chinacars Club (CCC) offers roadside assistance in a uniquely Chinese way: It relies on teams of red- and white-uniformed repair persons riding on battery-operated bikes to arrive on the scene within the promised 10 minutes, weaving in and out of heavy traffic without causing more air pollution. It offers standard AAA-like services too: leads for auto insurers and repair shops plus maps and discounts for merchandise. The site has rankings of suppliers that are based on customer evaluations—not comparable to the work done by the American research and consulting

firm J.D. Power but useful for first-time buyers. Then there's auto news compiled by 30 editors and staff members in 25 local branches with contributions from Chinacars' community of online members. Recent posts have included news about brake problems, maintenance tips, lists of the world's fastest cars, and an update on China's millionth Chery car to roll off a local assembly line. And don't miss the Web site's eye-catching photos of scantily clad girls posing with cars along with the colorful pop-up ads.

Chinacars leverages China's fast uptake of digital communications, leapfrogging past the old-fashioned AAA. To distribute a product mix that covers tires to spark plugs, Chinacars relies on the Web, mobile phones, call centers, and satellite transmissions to beam traffic info to drivers' navigational devices as they sit behind the wheel. Its snazzy Web site that sports a jazzy-looking logo is strong on Web 2.0 features that stand out on the red and black Chinese-language Web site. The interactive community features include tabs to blogs, an expert's corner, bulletin board systems, forums, and photos uploaded by members.

For those who prefer to get service the old-fashioned way, call centers are staffed by 150 representatives. If you're in China, you can dial 95156 to reach them. "Chinacars is an auto service portal, but in fact, it puts much effort into its offline business," says Tangos Chan of *China Web 2.0 Review*. "I think it is a typical successful case for a brick-and-mortar model in China."

The online business holds the most promise for this well-positioned company, which brings in revenues of $35 million and profits of $6 million. For a specialized site, Chinacars logs in at a hefty 23 million daily page views:

the number of times people click on a Web page. Jeremy Goldkorn at Danwei points out that Chinacars has hit a home run because, "Cars are a very popular subject among men in China, and men are the heaviest Internet users."

Growing competition is a potential speed bump, though. Goldkorn ticks off at least six rivals going after the popular auto service space. The large Chinese Internet portals Sina.com and Sohu.com have started their own automotive channels and have soaked up one-quarter of the $50 million in auto ads on the Web. A close competitor is the two-year-old United Automobile Association (UAA) in Beijing, which has 1.2 million members compared with Chinacars at 1.5 million (and the AAA at 43 million). In June 2007, UAA nabbed $21 million in venture capital from the top-tier firm Kleiner Perkins Caufield & Byers and the Chinese venture outfits Legend Capital and Ymer Venture Capital. Accelerating to stay in the lead, Chinacars recently teamed with China's Tom Online to provide rankings and online stores to its new partner's WAP (wireless application protocol or interactive channels on mobile phones) sites.

> "Cars are a very popular subject among men in China, and men are the heaviest Internet users."
>
> **Jeremy Goldkorn,**
> publisher, Danwei

Chinacars has piggybacked on the AAA idea, but it's strictly a commercial enterprise, whereas the AAA is a nonprofit organization with 66 profit-making chapters nationwide. There's no exact match to Chinacars in the United States, although it seems the full-service auto concept would work well in America. Automotive Web sites in the United States are more specialized than the full-service Chinacars. Autobytel.com is an online car-buying site, Edmunds.com is known as a resource for buying and selling vehicles, and eBay Motors is an auction-style market for buying and selling vehicles.

Like many other Chinese "returnees," Zhang has borrowed heavily from Silicon Valley's entrepreneurial culture to mold Chinacars. He used his *quanxi* (connections) to raise initial funds from the Wanxiang Group, the largest car parts maker in China, and then received $33 million from Goldman Sachs and Granite Global Ventures. As a motivational tool, Zhang granted stock options to one-third of his staff, who are looking to cash out when the firm goes public. A perennial issue he's faced is finding qualified managers to fill key posts. After long struggles to find experienced candidates, Chinacars recently picked off new chiefs of finance and technology from two Nasdaq-listed Chinese companies.

If Zhang can sustain the momentum, his next goal is Nasdaq. Zhang, age 47, has been prepping for this chance for a long time. The firstborn son of high-level Chinese bureaucrats, he went to the prestigious Institute of International Relations in Beijing to do undergraduate studies. In 1985, with a Ford Foundation fellowship in hand, Zhang, then 25 years old, landed at JFK Airport, his first trip to the United States. He spent a week in New York City and found the buzz of the city stimulating. He soon headed south on I-95 to the nation's capital, where the big monuments and stately buildings reminded him of his home city, Beijing. In the Washington, D.C. area for 10 years, he earned an MBA from Johns Hopkins University in Baltimore. His parents encouraged him to get a Ph.D. in political economy from the University of Maryland. While in D.C., his adopted hometown, he raised a family with his wife, a research assistant at Georgetown University Medical School. Leaving academia in 1995, he spent the next six years in top management positions at two Nasdaq-listed telecommunications firms. It was a good ride until the tech crash of 2001. That was when Zhang made up his mind to help shape China's new private enterprise economy.

Going for gold

His concept and timing for Chinacars couldn't be better. Cars and the Internet are liberalizing forces in the new China, and Zhang is going for gold. China's fledgling car market is growing by 36 percent a year and now includes 30 million automobiles, compared with the world's largest market, the United States, at 136 million. But most of those cars are owned by government agencies or corporations. The private car market in China is still small. Only about 3 percent of the population, or 13 million people, own a car; that's one of the lowest percentages of car ownership in the world. Sticker prices for cars are about 10 to 15 percent higher than they are in most places, putting autos out of reach for the masses. Most people ride bikes, take the bus, or, if they live near one of the few urban subway lines, ride the rails.

But private ownership is picking up. The watershed year was 2003, when individually owned cars surpassed taxis and government vehicles for the first time. By 2010, about 7 percent of the Chinese population will hold the keys to a car, the China Consumer Association predicts. This will put China way behind the American ideal of a three-car garage, but China is catching up in the number of driver's licenses. In 2006, 100 million Chinese—equal to one-third of the U.S. population—had a driver's license, according to the Chinese Association of Automobile Manufacturers, and the numbers are growing by double digits each year. The crowds gawking at auto showrooms in shopping malls and business centers are an indication of the interest. No wonder Detroit has arrived and quickly set up joint ventures to make Buicks, Fords, and Chevrolets even though China has yet to start exporting the cars it designs and makes to the United States.

Zhang is in the driver's seat as China seems destined to become the world's largest automotive market—the same place Henry Ford was with the Model T. Although not a car enthusiast, Zhang has to fit the part of auto exec, and so his wheels are a spiffy black BMW. Like many executives in Beijing, particularly returning Chinese with résumés packed with U.S. credentials, Zhang leads a comfortable life. He has a company car and driver waiting to take him to the office and back home. His apartment is in the Trump-like Palm Springs Villas next to Chaoyang Park in the northeastern part of Beijing, where expatriates prefer to reside.

Zhang is too busy to enjoy the surroundings much. He has the entrepreneurial habit of working nonstop and the backache to show for it. Influenced by his three years in Silicon Valley, he is motivated by its culture of rewards from commitment to a personal goal. This spirit of entrepreneurship is alive at Chinacars.

"In Silicon Valley, I saw that if you put your mind and heart into what you want to do and you do it with passion, that can be an incredible force," Zhang says as we meet one Sunday afternoon in a clubhouse at his apartment complex. We talk for two hours over tea, interrupted only by calls from his mother and then his wife, who has just arrived on a flight that afternoon from the Bay Area, where the family still has a home. Zhang speaks English fluently and, with his hair trimmed with Beatles-like bangs, could be a model in a J. Crew catalog. On that day he looked relaxed wearing a Johns Hopkins sweatshirt, jeans, and running shoes. He was on doctor's orders to get some exercise and had been walking around the well-manicured grounds complete with giant lion statues and fountains that would look more appropriate in Las Vegas.

If Zhang is in pain from the long hours leading his car troops, Chinacars is the beneficiary. It's speeding along at the pace of a hot rod, clocking in at 650 employees, up from 300 three years ago. In 2004, just three years after the starting pistols were fired, Chinacars pulled in $8 million in revenues and broke even. Revenues climbed to $13 million and profits to $2 million in 2005, then zoomed to $23 million and $4 million in 2006. The year 2007 was projected to bring in at least a 30 percent increase to revenues of $35 million and profits of $6 million.

The business model is constructed around auto buyers' needs. "We identified seven major needs, starting with a consumer who wants to buy a car. Then we go to car insurance, accessories, maps, repairs, and selling used cars. Then we close the circle and start again with the buying," Zhang says. "The market is too young to be segmented by each customer's need."

> *"In Silicon Valley, I saw that if you put your mind and heart into what you want to do and you do it with passion, that can be an incredible force."*
>
> **John Zhang,**
> president and CEO, Chinacars

Membership fees and online advertising, two fast-growing areas, provide most of the revenues. In the rear are referral fees from auto sellers and suppliers for sales leads, a tiny percentage currently, and the recently introduced e-commerce CareXpress service. In its first month, CareXpress got orders from 2,000-plus shoppers for car jacks, maps, tires, and other accessories; that's a respectable number considering that e-commerce hasn't caught on yet in China. People logged on to gawk at panoramic shots of the nearly 4,000 models available today in China.

Membership fees make up about 20 percent of revenues today but should increase as people begin to sample services that are new to China. There's an introductory free rate, but on average dues are $25 and VIP status costs $45. About half the site's revenues come from online advertising by automakers and suppliers such as dealers, repair shops, and insurance companies, many of them newcomers to marketing.

Zhang has had no shortage of power-packed investors who wanted to profit from his handiwork at Chinacars. He pulled in his first several million dollars in fall 2001 from a longtime personal acquaintance, the superwealthy Lu Weiding, CEO of China's largest automotive company, Wanxiang Group. Weiding became chairman of the board at Chinacars.

In light of the scope of his new business, the highly competitive environment, and the fast-paced marketplace, the disciplined Zhang has managed to raise venture capital sparingly, an indication that he has kept the burn rate (operational costs) low enough to keep going as the start-up expands. "Good start-ups put a strong emphasis on cash flow," says Zhang. "Surviving is all about cash flow and profits—growth and sustainable growth."

In October 2005, he landed overseas funding of $8 million from Granite Global Ventures (GGV), which joined Goldman Sachs in August 2006 for follow-up funding of $25 million. "It's an excellent company run by a great team of professional managers with the ability to deliver sustained growth," says David Chou, the Hong Kong–based managing director at Goldman Sachs. Thomas Ng, a cofounder and managing partner at GGV, boasts that Chinacars will become "not only the biggest auto brand in China but also one of the most recognized brands in the world."

The next milestone for Chinacars is to go public on Nasdaq. To gear up, Zhang recently hired a new chief financial officer—the third in six years—Jonathan Zhang (no relation), the former CFO of the recently Nasdaq-listed Chinese semiconductor firm Vimicro International Corp. His first CFO, Philip Feng, a high school classmate, left for Chinacars' first investor, Wanxiang. Zhang scrambled to replace him with an automotive research assistant Eric Wen from Morgan Stanley, who stepped in as CFO and chief marketing officer. Zhang also has a new chief technology officer, Alex Yi, a former vice president and the CTO of publicly traded Chinese start-up AsiaInfo Holdings, a referral from a friend after a search that lasted several months.

> "Chinacars will become not only the biggest auto brand in China but also one of the most recognized brands in the world."
>
> **Thomas Ng,**
> cofounder and managing partner,
> Granite Global Ventures

Road tour of Chinacars

One fall morning in Beijing I visit Chinacars, arriving there in the company car. It's in the heart of the city but looks like it could be in San Francisco's Mission District, home to dozens of dot-com start-ups during the Internet boom. We turn into a narrow alleyway, pass an old firehouse, and stop at a multi-story factory building with large casement windows. Riding upstairs to the offbeat headquarters in what used to be a cargo elevator, I land at a floor with a large, high-ceilinged open space loaded with young Chinese workers huddled in cubicles. It's an upbeat place. The color scheme is bright cherry-red offset by pure white. Red umbrellas festooned with the Chinacars logo are propped open for effect above the cubicle partitions. The hip, casual feel of the place is a refreshing contrast to the stuffy, heavy-draped offices of the state-controlled businesses I've visited.

Zhang bounds into the reception area with a big smile, gives me a brief tour of the space he designed, and escorts me to his double-level office. On the lower level is a conference room outfitted executive-style for boardroom meetings. In a loft above, reached by a steel staircase, is Zhang's office.

This is the place I imagine Zhang goes to plot strategy for Chinacars. Zhang honed his business skills at several challenging managerial posts at U.S. technology firms. Starting his professional career in 1995 as a management trainee at the Nasdaq-listed ADC Telecom Equipment, Zhang quickly was promoted to run ADC's joint venture in Shanghai. He made it profitable in one year. The next year, he was bumped up to president of ADC China, overseeing two joint ventures in Shanghai and Nanjing.

His break from corporate duty in China came in 1998, when he joined California Microwave Inc. in Silicon Valley as senior vice president for global business development, reporting to the CEO, Fred Lawrence. Zhang was charged with repositioning the firm more broadly in the booming market for broadband wireless access for high-speed Internet transmissions, but his timing was off. Later renamed Adaptive Broadband, the company saw its stock plummet in the tech slowdown that began in late 2000, and after two aborted acquisition offers, it went bankrupt in 2001.

Opportunity knocked when Beijing got the Olympics, and Zhang hopped on that flight to celebrate the historic occasion with his hometown friends and colleagues. Zhang might not have had the nerve to take the gigantic leap of starting Chinacars if it had not been for the support and encouragement of his wife and parents, who were all superstar achievers. His wife is a physician. His parents both worked at China's Ministry of Petroleum Industry, and his mother later became a doctor specializing in Chinese medicine.

Zhang's original concept for his start-up came from a service business modeled after the British company Virgin Telecom. He liked the fact that Virgin Telecom did not own a network but relied on mobile phone operators to resell its services under the Virgin brand name. Zhang realized that the key to this model was owning a customer base, providing services, and then getting recurring revenues. "I saw the opportunity to create this type of service in China, where I knew the market," he says.

He chose the AAA as his gold standard. "When I lived in the United States, I paid my AAA membership every year. I didn't think twice about it," Zhang says. He's still an AAA member and on a recent visit to the United States bought a pair of sunglasses at a 40 percent AAA discount. For myself. I gladly pay $60 annual dues for my AAA membership, which came in handy when I was stranded with a flat tire on my former VW, carburetor troubles on my Honda, and a dead battery on my Saab.

Passion plus

More than anything else, the critical factor for success in any start-up is passion, and Zhang has plenty. "Chinacars is what I really love to do," he says. "It is a tough job, but if you work hard and have a passion for what you do, you have a good chance of success."

Of course, it helps to keep the brain stimulated and the heart pumping when you are writing history the way Zhang is. Never again will he have the opportunity to create an entirely new service in a huge, newly opening marketplace. "This is a once-in-a-lifetime mission for all of us at Chinacars," he says with pride.

Judging from the revenues and profits Chinacars is generating and the creativity of its business model, it is likely that Zhang's start-up will be a household word in China the way AAA is in the United States. The site, with its blend of blogs, e-commerce, news, and membership services, might even be the model for a snazzier AAA. Chinacars has the most essential ingredient for success: the right CEO. Not too many heads of Chinese start-ups have Zhang's deep managerial and educational background or conceptualization of a business plan. After six long years of going at it with no break, Zhang and his team deserve the chance for a Nasdaq listing. Maybe they will make it happen.

If Zhang has competition for being the most determined entrepreneurial pioneer in China, it has to be Joe Chen, the crafty and wildly charging founder of Oak Pacific Interactive. Chen has the Chinese versions of MySpace, Facebook, YouTube, and Craigslist built into one power-packed collection of sites for Web-hungry youngsters in China. Personality plus, Chen calls himself "chief stickiness officer" for his task of keeping Web users glued to his site. He also has a new motto that sums up a lesson he's learned in his dash for first prize in China's Web world: "Less is more, fast is slow." Will his new measured approach work in keeping Murdoch on his toes as MySpace enters China? It might. It sure beats Chen's former half-crazy motto taken right from the lips of Steve Jobs: "Stay hungry, stay foolish."

CHAPTER FIVE

Imagine MySpace, YouTube, Facebook, and Craigslist rolled into one company. That's China's Oak Pacific Interactive. Now imagine Rupert Murdoch and his wife Wendi Deng making a run for your business with MySpace China. That's the card Joe Chen is playing at his social networking consortium with a public listing in the offing.

Oak Pacific Interactive— Web 2.0 on Steroids

Joe Chen sends his driver to pick me up from the Swissôtel where I'm staying in Beijing. He tells me to keep an eye out for a "Texas police cruiser." A beige-colored, plush-looking Lincoln Mercury Grand Marque pulls up, and I remind myself to ask Chen what he meant as we drive along a side road to avoid the clogged highways in the capital city's central Chaoyang business district.

It's a bright, sunny November day with a slight chill in the air: one of the few good seasons to be in the too-hot-and-humid or too-cold-and-dry climate of Beijing. Arriving at the entrance of a modern office building called China Life Tower that could as easily be in Chicago, I take the elevator up 18 stories to meet Chen. A colorful character with a maverick's personality, Chen is a grand dreamer and Internet pioneer who has mesmerized me with captivating yarns that blend philosophy, folktales, and common sense.

His rise from flipping burgers at Wendy's in Wilmington, Delaware, to earning a master's degree from the Massachusetts Institute of Technology and an

MBA from Stanford, along with his reputation as a Chinese Internet go-getter, make for a Clintonesque rags-to-riches story. Born in the central Chinese city of Wuhan, Chen, age 38, is chairman and CEO of Oak Pacific Interactive, a Beijing-based social networking company that is in the center of the hottest trend going: Web 2.0, online sites where a circle of friends chat, blog, share videos and music, send instant messages to one another, and play games online. His social networking powerhouse is an unparalleled collection of 11 sites, most of them modeled after successful Web 2.0 sites in the United States. Chen runs the Chinese wannabes of community network MySpace (Mop.com), video-sharing site YouTube (UUMe.com), networking portal Facebook (Xiaonei.com), and classified listings site Craigslist (RenRen.com). The master plan behind this grand scheme is quick gains and three big letters: IPO (initial public offering).

> *"The biggest problem for Oak Pacific is that it does not have a strong core business which it can sustain and scale."*
>
> **Tangos Chan,**
> publisher, *China Web 2.0 Review*

The disparate assemblage Chen has built through acquisitions and internal development in five years has served as a test for the CEO's ability to keep juggling without becoming overextended. Tangos Chan of *China Web 2.0 Review* says that Chen's performance could be better. "The biggest problem for Oak Pacific is that it does not have a strong core business which it can sustain and scale," he says.

In 2006, Chen raised $48 million primarily from Western venture firms and was gunning for an IPO with $7 million in profits and $50 million in revenues largely from advertisers drawn to some 200 million user clicks daily on its Web pages. But the start-up's small and shaky foundation, which is heavily reliant on mobile phone services, reversed the plan. A government regulatory change in the wireless service business cut into revenues; that resulted in financial losses and forced Chen to lay off 200 of the 800 employees. Now Chen needs to milk alternatives such as paid subscriptions and premium services. This is where his experience in keeping users glued to sites comes in handy. Chen calls himself the company's chief stickiness officer.

Chen soon will get to see how good he really is. Rupert Murdoch and his Chinese-born wife, Wendi Deng, are going after some of Chen's goodies.

Murdoch has put Deng in charge of strategy for launching the News Corporation–owned MySpace, the top U.S. networking portal, in China. This is Deng's first official role at the media colossus since she met Murdoch as a junior employee, became his Chinese interpreter and guide, and then his third wife in 1999. Deng, 39 years old, a native of the large eastern city of Xuzhou in Jiangsu province, has made several scouting trips to Beijing since the acquisition of MySpace in 2005 for a stratospheric $580 million. But critics and bloggers have blasted a trial MySpace China site and instant messaging service she debuted in spring 2007, claiming it's dull-looking in comparison to the eye-popping designs of most Chinese Web pages and lacking in features such as audio and video chat. Expect more fireworks in 2008 when Deng and her team of investors and managers roll out a full-scale MySpace China.

Chen and Deng are going after a potentially huge Chinese market for social networking. Today, young Chinese are always online, downloading music, posting videos, chatting, sending messages, blogging, and making up virtual personas. This is amazing considering the censorship and authoritarian control in communist China. Online advertising on Chinese social networking sites, with most of those sites trailing portals and search engines in obtaining advertising dollars, should hit $159 million by 2010, up from $23 million in 2006, forecasts the Shanghai-based iResearch Consulting Group. This is dwarfed by the estimated $900 million spent in 2007 for ads on MySpace, Facebook, and the like, in the United States, which is predicted to rise to $2.2 billion by 2010, according to the research firm eMarketer.

Chen discounts MySpace China's chances of doing it right in this hyper-growth market. But Chen will need all his hard-earned entrepreneurial experience to do battle with Deng, not least because of her mystique as Murdoch's confidante on all matters Chinese. With his early-bird advantage, parade of Chinese-language Internet brands, and millions of users, Chen essentially is ignoring latecomers MySpace China and Deng. Chen claims that Murdoch is "one of my role models" for building a global media empire but dismisses Deng with a curt, "I've never met her."

He's equally scornful of their new Chinese-language site. "I didn't even go on their Web site. They don't have a chance." He says he worries far more about fast-moving, well-entrenched local players such as Tencent Holdings' dominant QQ instant messaging service and an array of community-building services. "It will be impossible for newcomers to penetrate the fortress that smaller emerging players in China have built," he says, adding that home-grown companies have the advantage in China. The fast-moving, incredibly competitive Chinese Internet market requires quick decision making, on-the-ground insights, and flexibility to react to sudden changes in regulations or market shifts, he points out. "There are tremendous barriers of entry to the Chinese Net space," he says. "MySpace will be under pressure to do something revolutionary, something extraordinary."

In laying the foundation for MySpace China, Deng has picked up some lessons from eBay and Yahoo!. Unlike those multinational companies, which vainly struggled to customize services to suit Chinese users and ultimately turned operations over to domestic partners, she went local from the start. She's set up MySpace China as a Chinese company, separate from Murdoch's empire, with News Corporation owning a minority stake. Also, she's lined up high-powered managers and investors for the locally run Chinese site, which, like all sites operating in the People's Republic of China, is government-censored. To run the 36-employees-and-growing start-up, Deng's handpicked Luo Chuan, who ran Microsoft's MSN service for 12 years in China as CEO. As investors and majority owners, she's brought onboard IDGVC China, the well-regarded Chinese venture arm of the Boston-based International Data Group, and China Broadband Capital Partners, run by AsiaInfo founder Edward Tian. Deng is on the board, as are Luo, Tian, and MySpace co-founders in the United States, Chris DeWolfe and Tom Anderson.

Even with those big names behind it, industry observers agree with Chen that MySpace doesn't have a high likelihood for success. "Everyone thinks it's a total joke," says technology media publisher Jeremy Goldkorn. "It doesn't have a chance. The market is already really crowded, and they don't offer anything unique. The only thing MySpace China has going for it is News Corporation's deep pockets," he says, finishing with the punch line, "Deng has no experience in this field."

Chen doesn't have the best reputation either. Industry observers have accused him of inflating his numbers for lead site Mop.com, losing key managers because he's difficult to work for, and trying to manage too many Web sites at the same time. Moreover, Goldkorn says that Oak Pacific is skewed to a teen audience and pales next to sites with the older and richer demographic profiles advertisers prefer.

Yet few Chinese entrepreneurs can compare with the swashbuckling Chen for trial and error, success and failure. As a young boy growing up in China, Chen dreamed of winning a Nobel Prize in physics. But when he found he was not as smart as Einstein, he veered off into engineering and high-stakes entrepreneurship, becoming a multimillionaire as a student at Stanford University from an alumni networking start-up called Chinaren.com that he sold. He went on to fail at his next three stabs at tech start-ups.

He owes his risk-taking nature in part to immersion in the innovation culture of Silicon Valley. Like many Chinese tech entrepreneurs, he was influenced by the Valley's try-anything spirit and returned to his homeland to start something big just as the market was opening up. With his short, stocky frame and round wire-rimmed glasses, he doesn't look like one of the Valley boys, but he's picked up the lingo and can talk the talk. Take the line he borrowed from Steve Jobs and used as a sign-off on e-mails: "Stay hungry, stay foolish." He also worships Jack Welch and Warren Buffett. On his desk at the office are dog-eared books dense with underlining that chronicle their tales: *Icon*, *Winning*, and *The Warren Buffett Way*.

The house that Joe built

Lessons from those masters on innovation, leadership, and investment come in handy as Chen builds Oak Pacific in the fast-moving, high-risk Internet business. Moving quickly while the newly opened Chinese market is largely up for grabs, Chen has cobbled together his social networking house of brands quickly, brick by brick, with a cadre of top Chinese tech management talent. A pioneer, he cranked up his first social networking site in China in 2003, about the same time that MySpace's cofounders put the first pages of MySpace on the Web.

Chen realizes that opportunities to build an empire won't last long as more companies such as MySpace enter China, drawn by the country's booming wireless, Internet, and consumer markets. That's why he's in such a hurry, possibly to the point of overextension. Since 2003, Chen has raised $48 million from major venture capitalists, paid $35 million to acquire five sites in cash and stock deals, built three others from scratch using cheap Chinese software engineers, invested in another, and set up a joint venture with one more site.

"We gotta get big faster than rivals, and we're fairly fast in areas that really matter. We are land grabbing everywhere."

Joe Chen,
chairman and CEO, Oak Pacific Interactive

"We are betting very heavily on the future of the Net. The trend is an explosion of user-generated content such as digital photos, so we are capitalizing on that unlimited growth," Chen says. "Second, we are building content that can be easily delivered over the Net, and we are delivering copyrighted Chinese movies and sitcoms. Three, we are betting on wireless. We believe that in five to ten years' time, wireless will be more powerful than the personal computer. There will be a gradual transition to peer-to-peer communications networks in the wireless world, and when that happens, we will be there."

As we duck downstairs to grab a quick Subway sandwich in the basement lobby of his office building, an impatient Chen tells me, "We gotta get big faster than rivals, and we're fairly fast in areas that really matter. We are land grabbing everywhere. There is very little room to get really big in the United States, but in China, all boats are rising. Internet companies are experiencing 30 to 40 percent growth per year. The important thing is to focus like a laser on the best opportunities." Chen says he wants to build "the number one Internet company in China, worth some $30 to $40 billion in the next ten years."

I discount Chen's boasting as hyperbole because the largest Chinese firms are nowhere near that large. Only a handful of Chinese tech firms trading on Nasdaq have surpassed $4 billion in market capitalization, including search engine Baidu, instant messaging service Tencent Holdings, and solar company Suntech Power.

"There is very little room to get really big in the United States, but in China, all boats are rising. Internet companies are experiencing 30 to 40 percent growth per year."

Joe Chen,
chairman and CEO, Oak Pacific Interactive

Chen's master plan was going well until 2006, when he suddenly woke up with a financial nightmare and found himself cast as a "former Web 2.0 darling" in Chinese *Global Entrepreneur* magazine. Largely to blame were stiffer government regulations in the wireless communications market requiring, among other rules, that mobile phone users double-confirm purchases of games, ringtones, and music. Industrywide, mobile service slowed down. The ringtone seller Linktone Ltd. lost $3.4 million in the first quarter of 2007, and revenue and profits declined in 2006. The music and gaming company Hurray Holding saw revenues and profitability tumble in 2006 and early 2007.

No wonder Chen has adopted a new management mantra: "Less is more, fast is slow." To wit, he has quashed a plan to take Oak Pacific public in 2007 but says he may shoot for 2008. He also is cutting some mobile phone services and focusing on core Internet businesses. "The fisherman who is used to turbulent waters expects the waves and never flips. Then they catch the big fish when they come," says Chen, putting a folksy positive spin on the setback.

Chen may enjoy early-morning bass fishing expeditions and the occasional sea metaphor, but he has a long way to go before he lands the big one. "Bass fishing is like a start-up. You use your pattern recognition abilities to find good markets or fish," he says. Oak Pacific still needs a lot more bait to reel them in. Its leading brand, Mop.com, claims 30 million users compared with 126 million for MySpace in the much bigger U.S. pond. Moreover, Oak Pacific's revenues of $50 million compare with estimates of $525 million in 2007 for MySpace. On top of this, as many as 500 local Chinese sites are jockeying for position. "The online social networking space is still in the early stage," says Duncan Clark, chairman at the Beijing-based consultancy BDA China. "Leading players in the market have yet to secure entrenched market positions and will be threatened by new entrants."

Even so, his venture capital backers are betting heavily on Chen. "He's able to move fast because he's building a conglomerate of several sites, either through making them or buying them, and then he's integrating them," says David Chao, cofounder and general partner at DCM, a Sand Hill Road-based venture investor in Chen's firm. "Joe is always looking for the next big thing.

> *"Joe is always looking for the next big thing. He's looking for what's going to be top of the list two years from now; then he lays out a plan for the short to middle term."*
>
> **David Chao,**
> cofounder and general partner, DCM

He's looking for what's going to be top of the list two years from now; then he lays out a plan for the short to middle term."

Great survival instincts

If there's one quality in Chen that his venture capitalists treasure, it's his survival skills. On a follow-up visit with Chen a few months later, we sat at a local coffee shop for two hours as Chen related his fascinating life journey. Chen grew up in the populous industrial city of Wuhan, the geographic equivalent of Kansas City, the son of civil engineers who were sent to work in the countryside during the Cultural Revolution. He remembers summers so hot that he would sleep outside on a bamboo bed with mosquito netting. As a young boy fascinated with building model boats and airplanes, he fantasized about becoming a Nobel Prize winner in physics like Tsung-Dao Lee and Chen Ning Yang, who in 1957 became the first Chinese to receive that honor.

He was a junior studying physics at Wuhan University when his family got clearance to immigrate to the United States in 1989. They joined dozens of relatives outside Lancaster, Pennsylvania, where his uncle ran a mushroom farm and a supermarket. Within three days of landing, Chen got a job flipping burgers at Wendy's, but he soon quit to take English-language courses at a Delaware community college. By 1993, he had earned an undergraduate degree in physics from the University of Delaware at Newark, supporting himself by helping his father load trucks and deliver produce on weekends.

One of two students in his class to get into the Massachusetts Institute of Technology, he earned a master's degree in mechanical design theory in 1995, spending many hours in the library crunching numbers on FORTRAN computer programs. Thriving in an environment where Nobel Prize winners such as Dudley Herschbach hung out, he began studies for his Ph.D. He dropped out when he realized that his professors "were a lot smarter than I was" and that he had missed the heyday of physics since "there was more exciting stuff being discovered during Einstein's time."

Meanwhile, romance beckoned. After a multi-year transcontinental courtship and some 10,000 love letters, according to Chen, Chen's sweetheart from his hometown of Wuhan joined him in Cambridge, and they got married in 1995. Somehow missing the recruitment season for MIT grads, Chen looked for a mechanical engineering job through a career directory. He ended up in

Saint Joseph, Missouri, as a tech support manager at the family-owned Altec Industries, an old-line manufacturer that made hydraulic cherry pickers for utility trucks. "My wife and I were the only Chinese the town had ever seen who were not working in the restaurant or laundry business," he recalls. Altec soon sent him to China, where Chen designed products and then gravitated to sales, rising within two years to the position of a regional business manager.

Stanford tech elite

On a vacation in California, he visited the sunny campus Stanford University in Palo Alto, fell in love with the place, and made up his mind to apply to business school there. He was accepted and credits that to two strong hand-written recommendation letters from his bosses at Altec.

For Chen, going to Stanford was a dream come true in a place where the sky was the limit. He had saved nearly two years and used gains from lucky stock market picks to pay the tuition. The Web was taking off, and seemingly every Stanford student had a business plan in his or her back pocket, including Jerry Yang, who founded the Internet portal Yahoo! on campus in 1995. Chen decided that he had to have an idea for a business start-up too.

He launched an alumni networking site for Chinese students called Chinaren.com with two classmates, Nick Yang and Yunfan Zhou, who today run the Nasdaq-listed Chinese gaming company KongZhong Corp. Working his connections in the elite Stanford tech world, CEO Chen and his cofounders raised about $300,000 from 10 classmates. He also got intro-ductions to blue-chip investors and succeeded in nabbing $2 million from private equity titan Henry Kravis and $10 million from Goldman Sachs.

Chinaren.com became a leading Chinese portal within a year but burned through cash quickly. In late 2000, after Chen's 1999 graduation from Stanford, Charles Zhang, founder and CEO of the Nasdaq-listed Chinese portal Sohu.com and an acquaintance of Chen's from MIT, acquired Chinaren.com for $33 million. Chinaren.com was merged into Sohu.com right before the dot-com party ended early the next year. At Sohu, Chen was made vice president of strategy in China, but he bailed in March 2001, before his one-year contract was up. At his wife's urging, he held onto his Sohu shares, which were trading at $7. He cashed out three years later at $30 a share. He still thanks her for that advice.

Chen tried his luck once more, this time in Dallas, a high-tech hotbed loaded with engineers but not with entrepreneurs. He lent his business know-how to three start-ups. Working with a professor from the University of Texas (UT), he jumped into the hot fad of optical networking, or fiber for high-speed efficient Internet connections. Chen wrote a business plan in a month but didn't find any backers in the overheated sector of a weakened tech economy in the aftermath of the 9/11 terrorist attacks. Living off his savings in a rental apartment, Chen started an Internet security software firm with a local engineer but quit within three months when its customers didn't pay. His third start-up, which involved a low-cost chip designed by a UT prof for medical imaging equipment, didn't fly either.

The false starts convinced Chen that instead of depending on the product ideas of other people, he should rely on his own vision. With his savings from the buyout of his Stanford start-up depleted from $3 million to $200,000 in less than a year, Chen left Dallas and moved back to China in mid-2002 with a goal of building on what he knew best: social networking, which he learned about when he launched Chinaren. Inspired by the majestic and long-lasting trees on the golf course near his Dallas apartment, Chen originally called his Chinese start-up 1,000 Oaks Inc. Three years later he renamed it Oak Pacific Interactive to avoid confusion with a Los Angeles suburb and better reflect the firm's mission.

At the same time that Chen was pushing ahead, several other Chinese entrepreneurs had returned home to do Internet start-ups. The list included his Chinaren.com cofounders Zhou and Yang, who listed KongZhong on Nasdaq in 2004 and became multimillionaires. Leaping in, Chen wrote a business plan for a wireless version of an eBay auction site in China. In typical entrepreneurial fashion, he relied on a network of tech and venture contacts and friends and family to start it. Chen raised $240,000 from three angel investors in Dallas, $1 million from his former bosses at Altec, and $10,000 from his mother. He put in $100,000 of his own money after cashing in a small portion of his total shares in Sohu in early 2002; those shares had inched up $3 after sinking to a low of $1 in the tech stock drop in spring 2001.

But his wireless eBay didn't catch on among Chinese consumers, who preferred simpler services over the phone such as weather updates, news, and ringtones. Chen's mission seemed ill fated when his board vetoed his next idea: an online gaming company. It was time for his next act: a wireless portal for teens called Dudu.com, modeled on a popular site called Cyworld.com in South Korea, a market with a highly advanced Internet and mobile phone culture. At Dudu, which sounds like a horn honking but can be translated as "really fat" or even "running dog," adolescents can

chat, e-mail, and make up fake personas with fashions, hairstyles, and makeup they choose online. They also can get dating tips. Chen says the site was developed in-house in less than two months. "In China, we just chunk it out. We just do it," he says.

Getting big fast

When DuDu couldn't grow fast enough to compete, Chen picked up the pace in early 2004. He acquired an entertainment portal called Mop.com for $2 million in cash and stock, putting up $1 million himself from earnings and sales of his remaining shares in Sohu.com, which by then was trading at $30. Run by one guy, Tian Zhe, and 12 servers, Mop.com ("running cat") was an addiction among young teens for its chat, music, video sharing, and personalized Web pages. Chen immediately put 100 employees to work adding new features to the site. Users on Mop.com, which features a stylized cat logo, shot up from 9 million to 30 million.

As more Chinese Web sites entered the game, Chen upped the ante in late 2005 by acquiring an online dating site, UUMe.com. Founded by a close friend of Chen's, fellow Stanford MBA James Liu, UUMe.com had raised $5 million the year before from top-notch Silicon Valley players DCM and Accel, plus China's Legend Capital (notable for its investment in Lenovo) and Itochu Capital, a venture capital offshoot of the large Japanese trading conglomerate. Struggling to upgrade and attract more ads as a site for relationship advice rather than casual dating or sex, UUMe was repositioned as a YouTube-like video-sharing service. The video-sharing space is increasingly crowded, but Chen says he intends to "tough it out with a small team and small burn rate."

Using the $5 million, Chen acquired the tech blogging network DoNews.com (like Techcrunch in the United States), which is well known for a weekly roundtable program called 5G. He added WoWar.com, an online community for players of the World of Warcraft game, to the lineup too. He also inked a joint venture with an unnamed personal investor in Kuho.com ("Kool Monkey"), an online entertainment site for downloading music and videos. His one disappointment was being outbid in a deal to buy Douban.com, a site for exchanging book reviews, films, and plays.

The year 2006 saw no letup. Oak Pacific picked up $48 million in venture capital in a deal that Chen thought would never close. Funds were so tight that Liu and he bunked together in a no-frills Silicon Valley hotel that Chen found on Priceline.com. But the wait proved worth it. Suddenly Oak Pacific had a huge sum of money and stellar investors: UUMe's prior backers DCM and Accel, plus lead investor General Atlantic, a global private equity player based in Greenwich, Connecticut. It also had two new seasoned board members: DCM's David Chao and GA's Hong Kong-based managing director, Vince Feng.

Loaded with cash, Chen went on an acquisition and development binge. He started RenRen ("PeoplePeople" in English), an online classified listings site similar to Craigslist. He launched a social networking site for college students called 5q.com, ("me cute" in English). In the fall, he acquired its competitor, Xiaonei.com, a leading college social network Web site whose name means "on campus." Chen merged the two sites for 5 million registered users and says it's one of the firm's "best-performing sites so far."

If that isn't enough, Chen tested his first English-language site, Hi There, where online shoppers can design personalized logos in English for T-shirts, hats, ceramics, and other merchandise and then have the goods shipped to the United States from China. It's been made over as an online gaming site after being hit with unexpected import tariffs. To top off the year, Chen bought a 40 percent investment stake in a Chinese search engine geared for business users called Hylanda. He also expanded his firm's reach into online gaming, adding two sites—zgmop.com and ssmop.com—to its already popular pet.mop.com.

"We buy stuff, and then we integrate it and inject more resources after the acquisition," says Chen. "The acquisition is not just for revenues; it is for revenue potential." He adds that most of the firm's growth has come from innovative features the team has added to the sites it acquires.

Chen has made sure to surround himself with managerial talent in China, where a shortage of qualified candidates is a major issue. UUMe founder Liu, previously Chen's senior vice president and chief strategy officer, is today his co-chief operating officer, sitting within arm's reach of Chen in a shared executive office. His chief financial officer, Xiaoxin Chen, another alumnus of Stanford's business school program, sits diagonally across from Chen. Both Liu and Chen graduated in the top 10 percent of their class.

Chen brings in the founders of the sites he acquires, putting them in charge of their respective business units. The founder of Mop.com is now a senior vice president at Chen's firm. "We give them equity and vesting rights and high responsibility to do what they used to do and achieve their targets," Chen says. Keeping the entrepreneurial family intact is a lesson he learned from Sohu, from which Chen and his two cofounders bolted after it acquired Chinaren.

"I am applying what I learned in investment books: Buy companies of intrinsic value with a barrier to entry and then nurture them," Chen says. Among other sources, he's read and can recite from George Soros's interview in *The New Money Masters*, Sumner Redstone in *A Passion to Win*, and digital age luminaries Bill Gates, Jeff Bezos, and Larry Ellison in *The New Imperialists*. Chen says that after reading how both Redstone and Murdoch ran short on money in building their conglomerates, his biggest lesson is that cash is king. "I want to make sure I have an ample supply of cash to do deals," he says.

If there's one worry Chen doesn't have, it's capital. The $48 million venture sum he raised in spring 2006 gives him "a sense of freedom" and "flexibility to plan for the future," he says, adding, "We've been through bubbles before. This will help us be a long-term, viable company." What to do for an encore? "I want to build a company like Warren Buffett did with Berkshire Hathaway and use the same philosophy. The only difference is that mine is in the consumer Internet market."

When I chatted with Chen in Beijing a couple of months after the money hit the company bank account, he was looking relaxed and trimmer. He says he's been on a steady diet of oatmeal for dinner and routine visits to the gym most mornings. If he doesn't keep his weight in check, his wife gets to buy whatever designer goods she wants. Not that they have financial troubles. Chen and his young family live in a suburban-type luxurious housing development in Beijing. Chen even takes time for a Kodak moment as I snap photos of him standing proudly in front of his new Lincoln Mercury, the same model that patrolmen use in his adopted Lone Star state.

The last time we met in Beijing, it was May 2007. Chen was flying later that week to Santa Barbara for an informal gathering organized by his investors for the various companies in their portfolio. He also was planning to get close to Buffett by meeting the Chinese investor and former entrepreneur Yongping Duan, who successfully bid $620,000 for a chance to dine with the billionaire. He's even begun to think about what he might want to do once he's 50. "I'd like to try to figure out a way to make my dollars work harder, perhaps seed capital to bring more awareness to social issues," Chen says.

Meanwhile, Chen is trying not to obsess over his dream of IPO gold. He wants to go public so that he can have the cash to buy even more Web 2.0 brands in China and is impatiently eyeing a listing on Nasdaq or the Hong Kong and Shanghai stock exchanges in 2008. But with his new managerial mantra, "Fast is slow, slow is fast," he may have the discipline to let Oak Pacific ripen. "We want to break even on our long-term projects first and then go IPO," he says. He may not have the luxury of time. In five years, China's Internet market will go from adolescence to maturity, and leadership positions will be taken. "That will be the end of the game," he says.

Before we wind up the interview, I ask Chen what the most important ingredient for success in China is. He grins slyly and then answers, quoting Intel founder Andy Grove and his parable for success in business: "Only the paranoid survive."

I am counting on Chen to be among the survivors and have his shot at tech glory if he can stay focused and not stretch too much. He may not have the DNA to spot risks where others can, but that's what makes him the classic hard-charging, nonstop entrepreneur. In China today, it takes that kind of guts to make it. It also takes creativity and imagination, and Chen scores high there too. Being in the center of the action in the fastest-growing segment of Web communications today doesn't hurt either.

The next chapter profiles a Chinese entrepreneur, Fang Xingdong, who is equally passionate about what he is doing but must serve new masters who don't share his vision for his young company, Bokee.com. They kicked him upstairs until he fought back and regained his CEO title. Like Chen, he is going after one of the wide-open areas of the Internet today in China: blogging. He not only invented the Chinese word for blogging but set up one of the first blogging portals in this authoritarian, communist-controlled country.

China has an estimated 30 million bloggers—more than one-third of the world's total—thanks to the free speech crusader Fang Xingdong, who coined the Chinese term for blogging and set up that nation's first blog-hosting service. But censorship, regulatory crackdowns, poor management, and the lack of a clear business model are only the beginning of troubles for this fascinating start-up.

Bokee.com— Growing Pains

My first encounter with blogging was in summer 2002 at a Stanford University conference. Silicon Valley slowly was getting its mojo back after the dot-com era. A crowd was gathered at this event, which had been organized by the technology commentator Tony Perkins and his new media company, AlwaysOn, the successor to his tech publication *Red Herring*. Bloggers were seated in reserved center rows with their laptops open, furiously typing instant feedback to the speakers' remarks. Their comments were posted instantly on the AlwaysOn Web site and simultaneously displayed on a giant screen on stage. Soon, the Web logs captured more attention than the presentations. Even the speakers turned to them for cues.

It was all very engaging. Blogging was not going to be a fad, I told friends in New York City. They pooh-poohed the idea, pointing out that this "user-generated" medium would never replace professional journalists. Today, *The*

New York Times and *Newsweek* have blogs, blogging networks have sprung up, and bloggers such as the politico Arianna Huffington have become celebrities. Bloggers have clout and press credentials to cover presidential elections. From the appliance salesman to the next-door neighbor, blogging has moved from cult status to the mainstream. How do I know this? My mother in rural Ohio even got me a book on how to start a blog.

Blogging is a natural in a democratic country, such as the United States, founded on the principles of liberty and freedom of the press. After all, blogging is the freest form of expression on the Web today. Chinese youngsters have discovered blogging and love it, but the proliferation of blogs in China is a challenge for the government to police and also a threat. Pornography has been allowed to flourish online, but politics or religion have not.[1] Authorities have blocked controversial bloggers and shut down blogging sites.

Dozens of cyberdissidents have gone to jail for posting articles critical of authorities, according to Reporters without Borders. Rebecca MacKinnon, an advocate of free speech in new media and a journalism professor at the University of Hong Kong, says she knows of several bloggers who have been threatened. Those bloggers self-censored their comments, started a new blog with a different Web address, or stopped blogging for a while, she adds. "Chinese bloggers and blog-hosting businesses have viewed censorship as part of the necessary trade-off required for online speech," MacKinnon says.

But the blogosphere door is creaking open. One indication: A recent post criticized the mascot figure designs for the 2008 Beijing Olympics as silly and ugly. The designs were praised in government-owned Chinese media outlets.

Today, some 30 million Chinese are bloggers, accounting for more than a third of the world total.[2] Blogging first became popular on university campuses in China in early 2003, soon after it took off in the United States. I decided to investigate this phenomenon and set up an interview with a Chinese entrepreneur who played a key historical role in getting the commercial blogging business going: Fang Xingdong, the founder and creative spirit of Bokee.

Fang discovered blogging as a new media outlet in mid-2002, when his rants about Microsoft's dominance as a threat to the adoption of new media in China disappeared from online chat rooms on the Mainland.[3] A friend clued him in to the rise of blogs in the United States. He lay awake nights, pondering the possibility of starting a blog in China. By the end of the summer he had set up one of China's first blog sites, BlogChina, later renamed Bokee. Fang opened it with a zinger: "Each blogger is a world. Let everyone have their own blog." He even coined the Chinese word for blogging: *Bokee*, which also can mean "plentiful guests."

The number of people reading blogs in China has exploded to 65 million, or more than a third of the country's Internet users. Blogging first captured the public's attention in 2003, when a female blogger in southern China's Guangzhou with the alias Muzimei drew some 160,000 surfers to her site monthly with a vividly descriptive sex diary that featured her multiple partners. She even was featured in a *Time* magazine article.[4] In 2004, a Beijing blogger named Zhang Shihe drew attention to the new citizens' medium by breaking the story of a murder and posting photos of it, which local newspapers picked up. By May 2006, the most popular blog in the world came from China: a diary-like account written by a beautiful young actress named Xu Jinglei.[5]

Despite the outpouring of voices Bokee has ushered in, Bokee itself may not survive, says new media publisher Jeremy Goldkorn. He contends that Bokee lost its edge a few years ago when it moved from being a forum of personal voices and became a portal hosting anonymous bloggers. The arrival of Web portal SINA to the blogging scene in 2005 "blew Bokee out of the water" by signing up celebrity bloggers, he says. "I think Bokee blew its chance at the big time."

Yes, Bokee is in deep financial trouble and management turmoil. I've been briefed by two investors that Bokee may be about to go under. The company laid off about a quarter of its 400 employees and streamlined its blogging lineup in late 2005 and early 2006 but still lost $4 million in 2006. At the current rate at which it's burning through cash reserves, it will be out of money by the end of 2007. Meanwhile, the Chinese Web portals SINA and Sohu have sucked the air out of Bokee with competitive blog-hosting services. A search to find a revenue-generating business model for blogging—a problem for all sites—has not been successful. Also, Fang's leadership abilities are being questioned by his board of directors.

> "I think Bokee blew its chance at the big time."
>
> **Jeremy Goldkorn,**
> publisher, Danwei

I meet with Gary Rieschel, an investor and board member at Bokee, for breakfast at the executive club lounge of the Grand Hyatt in Beijing. Rieschel clues me in on the dynamics at play. "Xingdong is a very charismatic founder who is universally respected. He is talented, creative, and driven and has a passion for blogging and a passion for the business," says Rieschel.[6] "The commercial risk is that he is a CEO for the first time."

I arrive by taxi at the offices of Bokee in a run-down building dubbed Pioneer Park that is owned by nearby Tsinghua University, China's best entrepreneurial training ground. Tsinghua offers low rent and tax subsidies to start-up tenants. Bokee leases several floors of the six-story building. There's no elevator, so I climb three flights of stairs and find my way past rows of empty cubicles to Fang's tucked-away office. He's not there, the lights are dim, and the uncluttered office doesn't look occupied. This is my fourth visit to the start-up since fall 2005, and each time the Bokee chronicles are in more turmoil.

While waiting for Fang to arrive, I chat with the business development manager, Xin Wen, who goes by his English name, Kevin. A master's graduate of the University of Texas at Austin, Wen joined the team in early 2005 after his blogging site, BlogDriver, was acquired by Bokee. We're seated on a black leather couch, and above us is a framed Chinese character wall hanging. Wen says the script comes from an ancient Chinese classic text, which he translates for me as, "Strengthen self without stopping and hold world with virtue."

As I'm getting a feeling for Fang's character, I hear loud, fast footsteps heading toward the office. Fang bolts through the doorway, catching his breath, and we exchange greetings. Tall and slender, Fang, age 37, has a thoughtful face. His long bangs come close to his round glasses and make him look younger than he is.

The son of farmers, Fang grew up in the small Zhejiang province city of Yiwu, south of Shanghai, and graduated with a master's degree in electrical engineering from the Xi'an Jiatong University of Communications in 1994 in the inland city of Xi'an, the starting point of the ancient Silk Road and a tourist attraction for its life-size army of terra-cotta warriors and horses. He moved to Beijing to enroll at Tsinghua University as a Ph.D. student but dropped out during the height of the dot-com boom in 1999 to form China's first Internet consultancy and research firm, Chinalabs.

Intellectual, stubborn, and independent-minded, Fang quickly became one of the country's most influential information technology columnists. He was known for his outspoken critiques of the software giant Microsoft, including his 1999 book, *Arise and Challenge the Hegemony of Microsoft*. It's one of 20 books he's written, including a four-volume compilation of profiles and writings of the 100 most important information technology leaders and a tome about the history of blogging. This is an impressive array of accomplishments, all of which demonstrate that his drive has very little to do with getting rich.

Connecting with Fang

Wen acts as a translator because I don't speak Mandarin and Fang doesn't speak English well. Trying to make a connection with China's blogging godfather, I mention some of my new media contacts in the Valley. I'm struck by his links to the Bay Area. Fang has jetted to the Valley to attend the AlwaysOn conference twice, have lunch with Perkins in the Valley, and catch the latest issue of *Red Herring*. He also knows Dan Gillmor, a former tech blogger for the *San Jose Mercury News* who jump-started the blogging trend and authored a popular book, *We Are the Media*. His hero is Stanford law professor and author Lawrence Lessig, an influential advocate of open, free-ranging cyberspace.

I explain that I've heard about Bokee's latest woes and ask Fang to tell me what's going on. "We had a good vision, but we realize now that we need to take it step by step," he says. He acknowledges that his experience in running a company is "quite small" and that managing is a "big challenge." He also sheepishly admits that after Bokee raised the $10 million, "We didn't do a very good job." Leaning toward me, he says he wants to move from "high projections" to "more realistic actions." The translation is not perfect, but I get the point.

I ask Fang if the company is profitable now. No, he admits. Then he hurriedly adds that his goal "is to break even in six months, and then make some money in the next six months, and then go IPO." That doesn't sound step by step to me and doesn't jibe with what I've been told about his conflict with the board over his management. I ask him if he's still CEO. I figure he must be getting pretty annoyed by now, but he doesn't seem perturbed. He reluctantly admits that he's no longer in charge. A management committee, including his three key managers and himself, is running Bokee. He asks me to keep that information confidential even though I've already been alerted to this by close sources and by now it's a well-known fact. Fang says he's spending about half his time running Chinalabs, where he is incubating several start-ups.

Fast-forward self-destruct

The problems began to percolate when Fang turned to venture capitalists to finance his start-up. He raised $500,000 from Japan's Internet powerhouse Softbank Corp. in 2004 and $10 million the following September from three additional American venture capital firms.[7] Regulatory snafus almost prevented the funds transfer. The Bokee team spent two months without paychecks, waiting for clearance from newly issued regulations that required approvals for new investments from foreign entities.

Money in hand, Fang went into a self-destructive fast-forward. Without consulting his new investors, he hired 200 editors and technicians; that was a stretch financially even though the cost of starting a small business in China is substantially lower than it is in the United States. At the first board meeting, the new investors, who had a 30 percent-plus ownership stake in the start-up, had a fit and demanded that he lay off employees. One of Bokee's investors and former board members sums it up this way: "This company is all about emotion."

Bokee is feeling the pain from competitors. Bokee still claims to be the leading blog-hosting site in China with 13 million registered users, but SINA has gained market share quickly, according to blog publisher Chan of *China Web 2.0 Review*, and already claims as many as 6 million registered bloggers. Yet another new rival, the Shanghai-based Blogbus, raised $3 million in late 2006 from Chinese and Japanese firms.

Check-up and diagnosis

It's spring 2007, and I'm at Bokee to get the latest update. Fang is once again in charge even though my Bokee venture sources told me they would like to bring in an outsider to run the service. Fang spent the intervening time finishing his Ph.D. at Tsinghua University and running Chinalabs.

Two members of his core management team have resigned. Gone are chief operating officer Yongquan Tan, a Wharton MBA graduate who was recruited from Legend Capital in 2005, and chief technology officer Liang Lu, a Ph.D. from Texas A&M University who had been at Bokee for nearly three years after BlogDriver was snatched up.

On the plus side, in May 2007 Bokee survived a regulatory scare that would have required bloggers to register their real names. That could have destroyed the appeal of blogging in a country just beginning to get a taste of the power of personal expression.[8]

Start-ups mean suffering

Clearing his throat before answering, Fang puts an emotional spin on the management shake-up. "The bad timing made people stronger, but not strong enough for the tough times. Doing a start-up can mean a lot of suffering," he says. "The only happy moment was in 2005, when we hired people." I ask Fang how much money Bokee lost in 2006. I don't expect him to answer, but he does: $4 million. Revenues could not keep up with the high cost of running the place, but it remains to be seen if Fang has learned his lesson.

> "The bad timing made people stronger, but not strong enough for the tough times. Doing a start-up can mean a lot of suffering."
>
> **Fang Xingdong,**
> founder and CEO, Bokee.com

With any start-up, the best indicator of success is the commitment of the CEO. Fang wants to make sure that I understand that he is on the job and ready to put his heart and soul into getting Bokee back in action. Six months earlier, he acknowledged that he was more interested in fostering the development of start-ups through Chinalabs than he was in Bokee. This time, he confides, he's on the case. As proof, he tells me he was up until 4 a.m. the night before talking with his wife about what he should do about Bokee. His wife, who runs her own public relations firm in Beijing, encouraged him to turn up the heat on sales and "go get deals." Fang says he is reinvigorated by the discussions. "I am starting with that today for the long-term future. I want to make my company an influential company in China," he says. "We can survive if the team can work together."

Fang has turned over the management of his pet project Chinalabs to cofounder and new media expert Junxiu Wang. He's cut back his blogging to twice a week. I ask if he's hired a new CTO yet. No, he hasn't. Who's taking the place of former COO Tan? Fang says that Tan has turned his job over to business development manager Wen.

If Bokee is going to make it, what are the revenue-generating ideas? Fang says Bokee can eke out a profit this year. He is looking to online advertising and partnership deals with telecom companies for revenue streams. Wen clues me in with two examples. He points to Bokee partnerships in several local provinces with two Chinese phone companies—China Telecom and China Netcom—where subscription-based services such as photo sharing are bundled with the two Chinese phone companies for fees ranging from $1 to $3 monthly. He also cites a major deal in the works in which Bokee's blogging platform will be embedded in the operating system in China for a multinational cell phone maker. I notice that this time Fang has not brought up the prospect of going public. That scenario is highly doubtful now.

Such drama in entrepreneurial circles in Silicon Valley was common during the dot-com period: Passionate, committed, charismatic founder starts leading-edge business, needs money to expand, brings in an experienced group of venture capitalists, and soon inherits a board of directors that doesn't share his vision for taking the business forward. The fact that this is happening in China says much about how far the economy has progressed toward making entrepreneurship a central driving force. It is also is a valuable lesson for other Chinese entrepreneurs who are considering taking on outside investment: Make sure everyone is in agreement about the vision and the strategy so that budgets can be set accordingly.

To make sure I have the full story, I set up a follow-up interview with former COO Yongquan Tan, who used to be my key source at Bokee. Tan starts off by taking full responsibility for the company's mishaps: "I sacrificed for three years and I learned a lot, but I wasn't able to take this company to success." He did succeed in attracting approximately $2 million in online advertising from big-name clients IBM, Amazon, and Hewlett-Packard. Also, he lured in the telecom companies Nokia, Samsung, and China Mobile, charging them a fee for wireless blogging services such as uploading photos taken with a camera phone to Bokee's site. He also brought in subscriber fees for premium content such as big-name columnists.

Another initiative was Bokee Bank, modeled on the innovative South Korean blog site Cyworld, which was introduced in August 2006. It attracted 1 million new bloggers and brought in about 10 percent of revenues. Under the virtual currency system bloggers on Bokee charge their readers, Bokee takes a 20 percent cut of the fee, and writers use their earnings to pay for products and services online. It's an idea that could work in the United States too.

I come away with the impression that Bokee's opportunities for money-making ideas are limited. Most online advertising is centered on the top Chinese portals, with specialized car, housing, and consumer goods sites getting the leftovers, he says. Advertisers have not flocked to blogging sites in China or the United States. Membership fees are an iffy source; most blogs are free. Charging for VIP premier services is a possibility, but only block-buster features get people to pay up. Another avenue is fees for blogging over mobile phones, but that requires working closely with the monopolistic phone networks in China to reach mass scale. One experimental model— charging advertisers for referrals from the Bokee site—could blossom. Tan mentions that the automaker Ford tried out a participatory blogging and advertising campaign for a car launch last summer that worked well.[9] He sees opportunities for other targeted ad campaigns to work but cautions that for such a referral program to pay off, "You need a user base that is large and sticky."

A work in progress

Log on to the Bokee site and the vibrant home page appears, loaded with pop-ups and streaming text, brightly colored subject headings, and sections for news, blogs, and music and audio files, accompanied by a dashing bright red logo. There are subject tabs for technology, culture, society, and economy and an online community section for podcasts, photos, and music and video exchanges. But the business plan is still very much a work in progress. "You can raise large sums of money," says AlwaysOn's Perkins, "but you need a business plan that works."

Perhaps the most telling indication that Bokee is in trouble comes from one of its original backers, Granite Global Ventures. The venture firm is hedging its bets on Bokee by investing $10 million in late 2005 in a rival site, the three-year-old Chinese blog-hosting company BlogCN. The main difference between the two rivals is that BlogCN is more focused on online communities where friends can upload and exchange videos, photos, and music, whereas Bokee is more news-driven, explains managing partner Jixun Foo. He took a board seat at BlogCN, and his colleague Jenny Lee stepped off the board at Bokee. When I meet Foo in Shanghai at a local coffee joint, he acknowledges that "it is hard to tell" which blogging approach will gain the most traction in China.

I then arrange to go to Hangzhou to meet with the founder of BlogCN, 28-year-old Hos Ku, a computer science and engineering graduate from Hangzhou University and former manager of the Nasdaq-listed Chinese Internet firm NetEase.com. Ku invites me to a private dining room at a local seafood restaurant and fills me in on his firm's short history. He tells me how he formed the company at his apartment with two young engineers in July 2004 and built it to 180 employees and 10 million registered users. His next major project is to launch blogging over mobile phones. It sounds good, as do most Chinese entrepreneurial tales—at least on the surface.

For Bokee, the true test of survival comes now. I doubt Bokee can weather another wrenching transition. I admit I am rooting for Fang because I like and admire him. Whatever happens, Fang will have made his mark on Chinese new media history by helping to spread the power of blogging. If Bokee does go under, it will not be good for the flow of ideas that has bubbled to the surface in China through blogging. As the China media expert MacKinnon puts it, "Blogs are creating an independent space for discourse, interaction, and collaboration." She says that blogs "can contribute to major sociopolitical change in the long run" and that a "new generation will debate public affairs, engage in critical thinking, and be more ready for reasoned self-governance."

The next chapter leaves the entrepreneurs who are creating China's future and deals with the venture capitalists who are funding it. After vowing they would never fish for promising start-ups beyond the Valley ecosystem, top American venture capitalists have filled business-class seats on planes to Shanghai and Beijing. They are hoping that the entrepreneurial spirit and leading-edge innovations they bred in the Valley during the dot-com era will come alive in China and that they will find the same dreams, aspirations, and ambitions there. Together with a new crop of Chinese venture investors they are looking not for copycats of Google, Amazon, Yahoo!, and MySpace but for true innovators—the promise of the next new thing. The next chapter is the story of their eastward journey and their quest for breakthrough technology in the Middle Kingdom.

 part two

THE VENTURE CAPITALISTS

Follow the money trail directly from Sand Hill Road to Beijing and Shanghai, where California's best venture capitalists are looking for a pot of gold among China's homegrown entrepreneurs and their innovative start-ups. With an avalanche of American money looking for original technology, the Chinese copycats are being upstaged.

Silicon Valley's Tech Route to China

I'm driving a convertible with the rooftop open, enjoying the sun and the scenery while heading south on Route 280 from San Francisco. The Pacific Ocean is just over the grassy ridges of the Santa Cruz Mountains to the west. At Sand Hill Road, I end up at Sequoia Capital amid manicured lawns, towering redwood trees, and blossoming roses.

Don't be fooled by the perennial sunshine; this is the western Wall Street. Fueled by the Internet revolution and nearby Stanford University, this venture epicenter has created more wealth in a shorter time span than any other place in history. This potent mix of finance and technology in Silicon Valley produced Google, Cisco, Oracle, Palm, Yahoo!, Apple Computer, and Amazon.

I'm here to meet Don Valentine, a godfather in this valley, who founded Sequoia Capital in 1972. Valentine drives a red Mercedes convertible and at 75 years of age is aging-movie-star-handsome with a silvery head of hair, a square jaw, and confident body language.

When Valentine talks, people listen. Now, in a conference room, Valentine is offering me his bleak view of China. China is too far and too foreign. It's crippled by ills such as intellectual property theft, immature stock exchanges, and regulatory problems. Sequoia has made its stellar reputation by nurturing young companies within a 50-mile radius—driving distance from its office. It incubates promising start-ups upstairs, where the partners coach and mature fast-growing tech seeds, working hands-on with immigrants, first-generation Americans, and underdogs—Sequoia's favorite kinds of people. As if on cue, the young founders of a start-up team pass by the meeting room. They are giggling. "I hear laughter," says Valentine, "so it must be good."

My meeting with Valentine was in spring 2003, and a lot has changed since then.

Today Sequoia is deeply invested in China. It is searching there for the next tech innovation that will thrill consumers, rock the public markets, and enrich the firm with sales of skyrocketing shares—a hit on the order of the Palm handheld digital organizer and its staggering opening-day valuation of $53 billion in the hyped-up public markets of early 2000. Only about 8 percent of China's gross domestic product comes from high tech now, but the government's latest five-year economic plan is ushering in change with its emphasis on technology as a cornerstone of growth. Soon China—long known as a low-cost manufacturer—could be respected for innovations too.

Digging for gems in China, Sequoia raised a $210 million China fund in 2005 and planted Sequoia Capital China in Beijing and Hong Kong. Two more funds budded in spring 2007: $250 million for start-ups and $500 million for fast-growing companies. Suddenly, Sequoia had nearly as much gold-digging money in China as in the United States.[1]

In less than two years, Sequoia's 13-member team led by two Chinese prospectors, Fan Zhang and Neil Shen, has invested in 27 would-be digital stars: streaming media broadcasters, online ad services, social networking sites, and wireless search and video-sharing start-ups, among other software, semiconductor, gaming, and Internet deals. Young, savvy, and arrogant, Shen, a master's graduate from Yale, took online travel portal Ctrip.com and Home Inns economy hotel chain public onto Nasdaq, and Stanford MBA Zhang, a former investor at DFJ ePlanet Ventures, financed the Nasdaq-listed search engine Baidu and online game player KongZhong Corp. With nearly $1 billion to invest, Sequoia has one of the largest wads of cash of any U.S. venture firm in the People's Republic of China (PRC).

The money trail leads directly from once-parochial Silicon Valley to China, with emerging market India another favorite destination in the $32 billion increasingly global venture capital market.[2] Chinese venture funds soared from $3.4 billion in 2006 to $3.7 billion[3] in the first half of 2007, nearly half for all of Asia in 2006. China nudged up to the U.S. funds of $6.4 billion in mid-year 2007 (see Table 7.1).[4] Another indicator of the momentum: In 2006, 112 Chinese start-ups got venture financing,[5] more than double the 54 in 2005.[6] Fueling the momentum were China's giant initial public offerings, the world's largest in 2006.[7]

Not as much investing frenzy has been seen since the tulip bulb craze in seventeenth-century Holland or, in more modern times, the Internet bubble of the late 1990s. Both surges came to a crashing halt. Billions were lost in the dot-com bust as companies with high-priced stock such as portal and broadband provider Excite@Home went bankrupt. Initial public offerings of venture-backed tech companies fell from 229 to 37 between 2000 and 2001.[8] The fact that investors see China as the next big trend is in itself a warning sign: Japan was the hot market 25 years ago, and Eastern Europe followed it.

It is a little early to tell if the current heated climate for deal making is a repeat of the irrational exuberance of the Internet bubble in the United States. Preliminary indications are that China funds will do okay but probably will not come near the triple-digit financial returns of the top-tier U.S. technology

	CHINA	ASIA	UNITED STATES
2003*	$210	$2,372	$9,912
2004	641	4,772	17,890
2005	2,169	10,956	25,352
2006	3,409	11,973	24,730
First half 2007	3,650	7,514	6,360

*Figures are in US$ millions.
Source: For China and Asia, *Asian Venture Capital Journal*; for United States, Dow Jones VentureOne.

Table 7.1 China Venture Funds Rush In: Amounts Raised to Invest in Start-Ups

funds during the boom times in the Valley, when practically every new tech deal turned to gold. So far, a few funds that began to invest early in China, beginning in about 2002, have managed to turn in respectable performances of 20 percent. Successful investments in well-timed standouts such as Baidu and Alibaba helped.

Going forward, the challenge is to strike it rich with newer, unproven investments from a fresh crop of mostly local entrepreneurs. Most Chinese venture firms are predicting strong net returns north of 25 to 30 percent for their China technology funds,[9] but there is little proof of that yet aside from good progress in their portfolio companies. And there are a lot of ifs: The possibility that the surging Chinese economy will collapse is just one of the many hazards in the already risky, highly cyclical venture business. In the dot-com bust earlier in this decade, average returns for venture capitalists fell to about −5 percent. In light of the fact that most American venture players are new to China, emerging Chinese entrepreneurs are untested, and valuations for hot deals are going sky-high, in-the-know industry executives predict that probably only a few China funds will score above a 20 percent return to investors.

The money for these new Chinese funds comes largely from U.S. institutional investors and wealthy individuals. They have bought into the China economic growth story and the skyrocketing IPOs from early successes such as Baidu. At an annual meeting of Venture TDF in Shanghai's Four Seasons Hotel, I chatted with a group representing the Rockefeller family, managers from the giant U.S. pension fund CalPERS (California Public Employees Retirement System), representatives of the Stanford University endowment, and financial advisers to many other U.S. groups. We were treated to economist briefings, speeches by local media celebrities, and a dinner at the private mansion of real estate mogul Vincent Lo, developer of the swanky Shanghai Xin Tian Di shopping and residential complex.

More big American institutional investors have lined up at China's door in the last two years. Massachusetts Mutual Financial Group recently put $130 million of its $2 billion in private equity investments to work in Asia funds, with China ventures at the forefront. Managing director Mike Hermsen, who oversees the insurer's growing pool of money for Asia, says, "China offers among the best attractions in the world as a market for venture capital. It has the population, culture, ambition, and desire to create wealth."

Today, the Valley is on the tech route to China. No longer funding the copycat start-ups they once did, new venture explorers are searching to find and fund a breakthrough idea in China with intellectual property that can disrupt technology standards, establish a new paradigm, and possibly go global. The rewards increasingly are cutting-edge technology developed by homegrown Chinese entrepreneurs— raw, energetic, and unproven—and riding on the nation's rapid ascent in digital media, wireless communication, and science. For investors looking to reap extraordinary gains, China and its energetic people offer the prospect of profitability and perhaps the "next big thing."

"Everyone talks about corruption in China, but I have found Chinese entrepreneurs to be so honest, fair, real straight, and tough on themselves."

Morten Lund,
cofounder, LundKenner,
and early investor in Skype

Morten Lund, the visionary Danish investor who discovered and made Skype a hit with its free chat and text service, has a global perspective on technology development. Today he backs five Chinese tech start-ups. "Everyone talks about corruption in China, but I have found Chinese entrepreneurs to be so honest, fair, real straight, and tough on themselves," he says.

Tom Byers, a Stanford professor of entrepreneurship and the author of a popular technology ventures textbook, often is asked what the secret of Silicon Valley's success is. Today he sees the financial, cultural, and educational infrastructure that created the Valley rising in the People's Republic of China. Says Byers: "China has the best shot at replicating the Silicon Valley model of the next 50 years."

Of course, Chairman Mao Tse-Tung never anticipated that Red Guards, teenagers who during the Cultural Revolution marched through the streets denouncing the "running dogs of Wall Street," would see today's entrepreneurs courting venture capital from the United States. This new generation, even under the ominous shadow of the former leader of the Communist Party of China, seems more interested in following the advice of Mao's successor, Deng Xiaoping: "To get rich is glorious!" Not since the Marshall Plan for rebuilding Europe and repelling communism after World War II has such a huge economic transformation been launched.

China seductions

China's riches are largely untapped by venture investors, and Sequoia's Don Valentine is far from the only big-timer along Sand Hill Road who has been swayed by its seductions. John Doerr, the slender, hard-wired partner at Kleiner Perkins Caufield & Byers, blasted into China after his partner Ted Schlein went on a fact-finding tour of the Middle Kingdom and reported back to Menlo Park, in the fashion of the thirteenth-century explorer Marco Polo, about the incredible advances he had seen.

In April 2007, Doerr held a press conference in Beijing and broke the news: Kleiner was digging for the next big idea in China, its first outpost since the firm was founded in 1972 by engineers-by-training Tom Perkins and Eugene Kleiner. Doerr told reporters that Kleiner was heading eastward, bringing its Valley success formula to emerging tech companies in China. Let the search begin for the next Jeff Bezos, Sergey Brin, or Bill Joy in China. Schlein heartily endorsed the plan.

> "On a global scale, the pace of innovation is increasing, and China is helping lead the way."
>
> **John Doerr,**
> partner, Kleiner Perkins Caufield & Byers

"On a global scale, the pace of innovation is increasing, and China is helping lead the way," he said.

Kleiner began raising its first China fund, weighing in at a hefty $360 million, more than half the size of the firm's latest U.S. fund at $600 million. Two impressive and well-connected Chinese venture capitalists, Tina Ju from TDF Capital and Joe Zhou from Softbank Asia Infrastructure Fund, were picked to set up KPCB China in Shanghai and Beijing with a core team of seven.

Go down the list of the Bay Area's venture players—New Enterprise Associates, DCM, Draper Fisher Jurvetson, Sutter Hill Ventures, Venrock, Mayfield Fund, Accel Partners, Granite Global Ventures, Charles River Ventures—and nearly all of them have a China strategy. For most, this is their firm's first overseas location.

The downside

Not everyone is convinced that China is a good place to put money. Higher-quality deals, better-qualified entrepreneurs, and superior returns explain why the United States remains the favored destination, according to a Deloitte & Touche survey. China has many dangers, including the risk of political turmoil and the possibility that Deng's legacy of embracing capitalism may transform into a less hospitable business climate. For business, continuity and consistent rule of law are vital.

Asian-American Guy Kawasaki grew up in Hawaii and might be expected to be a China evangelist, but no. When he isn't writing books about empowering entrepreneurs, Kawasaki runs Garage Technology Ventures, and nearly all the 40 start-ups in his portfolio are in California. "Why would I want to invest in China when venture capital is difficult enough in the United States?" he asks.

It is a good question. Joel Dreyfuss, editor-in-chief of *Red Herring* magazine, highlights 100 winning Asian start-ups each year, and 40 of the 2007 lot came from China. But Dreyfuss says he sees more "me-too China businesses that copy U.S. models and not all that many original ideas." China, he adds, still is seen largely as a low-cost manufacturing center and a huge market, not a research and development center. "I think it will be another 20 years before China moves up the value chain and reaches critical mass in cutting-edge technologies," he says.

> "Why would I want to invest in China when venture capital is difficult enough in the United States?"
>
> **Guy Kawasaki,**
> managing director,
> Garage Technology Ventures

Even the biggest risk takers in the Valley have backed off from taking calculated gambles in China's hard-to-fathom legal and financial landscape. For starters, foreign venture capitalists typically need to detour to a tax haven such as the Cayman Islands and inject the assets of their Chinese start-ups in a WOFI (Wholly Owned Foreign Investment) structure. This lets them take their portfolio companies public on Nasdaq or the New York Stock Exchange and realize a profit in U.S. dollars instead of the nonconvertible Chinese currency.

Those contortions have been reinforced by a series of regulations and guidelines from China's Ministry of Commerce and State Administration of Foreign Exchange in recent years that have variously tightened and loosened the rules. Consider the fact that WOFIs with Chinese citizen shareholders must be registered and approved, and most are, since equity stakes are a key financial motivator for entrepreneurs to build businesses. Or think about this: Chinese entrepreneurs must pay for stock options and deposit the proceeds from selling shares in a start-up to foreign-currency bank accounts in the PRC. In part, the laws are intended to make sure that China gets tax income from money made by Chinese citizens in domestic companies. Another hurdle is immature capital markets for taking a venture-financed company public, though rising prices at the Shanghai and Shenzhen bourses are creating a new but still volatile exit route.[10]

"I think it will be another 20 years before China moves up the value chain and reaches critical mass in cutting-edge technologies."

Joel Dreyfuss,
editor-in-chief, *Red Herring*

Also, the long flights and "pain points," to use a Silicon Valley expression, may not be worth it. So far, there's not enough evidence that this latest burst of deal making in China is paying off. Fifteen of the twenty-two Chinese companies that went public on Nasdaq or the New York Stock Exchange in 2005 and 2006 were venture-capitalized tech firms, but most were backed earlier this century and don't represent the new breed of innovation investments.

Partners at the giant New Enterprise Associates (NEA) are disappointed that among some 18 investments in China since 2002, only 3 semiconductor firms have gone public, says partner Scott Sandell, who leads the firm's China activities. NEA put a hold on China investments in midyear 2007 while it worked through a backlog of deals ranging from online dating services to satellite broadcasting providers. "Returns from China have been more difficult than we originally anticipated," he says.

But there has been a clear symbolic shift from the early 1990s, when the pioneers of Chinese venture capital sweated to earn back money in investments troubled by corruption, fraud, and financial disputes. Most of those investments were in ill-fated joint ventures or state-owned enterprises, which then were the only pathway to China.

China pipeline

Two prominent early adventurers into China—Ta-lin Hsu of H&Q Asia Pacific and Lip-Bu Tan of Walden International—offered a welcome mat to China for their Sand Hill Road colleagues to get comfortable with the Middle Kingdom. At home with the customs, language, and culture on both sides of the Pacific, the hard-driving but charming Hsu and the smooth-as-silk mannerly Tan shuttled from San Francisco to Beijing and beyond painstakingly doing deals, earning 1K frequent-flier status, and becoming regular guests in the United Airlines Red Carpet Club at gateway cities.

Tan, a Malaysian-Chinese Singapore native, started Walden in 1987 to invest in cross-border Asian-U.S. deals after his doctoral studies in nuclear engineering at the Massachusetts Institute of Technology were derailed by the Three Mile Island nuclear leak. He raised a China fund of $100 million in 1994 that barely eked out $120 million, largely because of blatant corruption that led him to walk away from deals and sell shares back to management when disputes erupted over bookkeeping or accounting. In 2000, he landed his first in a string of China hits when the Chinese Internet portal Sina.com went public on Nasdaq.

The Mainland China-born Hsu grew up in Taiwan, got his Ph.D. in electrical engineering from the University of California at Berkeley, and founded H&Q Asia Pacific in 1986 to invest in Asia and the United States after a 12-year tenure as a researcher at IBM. Hsu helped jump-start Taiwan's high-tech industry and brought Starbucks to China, recently selling the Beijing and Tianjin franchise for a "very good" return to the Seattle-based parent company.

But Hsu remembers all too well the protracted legal battle he fought along with HSBC Holdings and New York Life Insurance over a land title in an expatriate housing and golf course development project called Shanghai Links, a $50 million investment in 1997. Nearly 10 years later, in 2006, after an award of

$66.5 million in damages over the land lease in 2001, the investors got clear title from the sellers of the high-end property, recouped some $10 million in legal costs, and got the Chinese government to absorb the back taxes. Now Hsu and his coinvestors are looking to sell Shanghai Links for the right price.

With such nightmares in the past, Hsu and Tan soon started ushering Sand Hill Road Hill to China. They let three firms—NEA, DCM, and Oak Investment Partners—in on one of their treasures: a trend-setting Chinese chipmaker called Semiconductor International Manufacturing Corp. led by the Taiwan semiconductor legend Richard Chang that was set to duplicate Taiwanese expert chip production in Mainland China. In 2003, the three American firms participated in a $600 million funding for SMIC as part of a huge $1.5 billion financing that brought in Walden, H&Q Asia Pacific, and Goldman Sachs.

SMIC went public on the New York Stock Exchange the next year. Though the stock's early prices were disappointing, SMIC shares gradually traded higher, eventually providing the early investors respectable profits. The word went out: China was an okay place for American venture dollars.

The herd instinct kicked in in spring 2004 when the financial service provider Silicon Valley Bank (SVB) hosted an invitation-only China tour. Some 25 top players from the Valley, including Valentine and Doerr, made the one-week whirlwind tour of Beijing and Shanghai to get a China briefing with local entrepreneurs, executives at public companies, and government officials. They came back in awe of the market potential and the Chinese entrepreneurial machine. Fast-forward one year, and SVB had opened up a branch in central Shanghai, providing with its investment banking services an important part of the ecosystem needed to foster entrepreneurship. Several American firms soon put their nameplates at the SVB location too.

American venture newbies to China went local fast. DFJ's Tim Draper swallowed a taste of snake blood as a Taoist medicinal regimen, Accel's Jim Breyer took lessons in Mandarin, and Len Baker of Sutter Hill took a river tour of the Three Gorges. Some unnamed venture capitalists took a liking to certain nightclubs in Beijing and Shanghai where the story I'm told is of shenanigans with local hostesses.

That infatuation might have occurred even earlier if it hadn't been for the outbreak of severe acute respiratory syndrome (SARS) in spring 2003. Fear of the virus sent Americans scurrying back to the safety of California, where they kept their distance from Mainland Chinese entrepreneurs who had escaped to the Valley. China deal making went dead.

One of my most memorable times in China was at the height of the SARS scare. I was in Shanghai. A get-together for the Palo Alto firm Focus Ventures was canceled, and a *Red Herring* conference had only about a dozen attendees, all comparing notes on what precautions to take. I holed up in the Hyatt Hotel overlooking the Bund, about the only foreigner left in the hotel. After a thundery night at the Hyatt, with lightning hitting the support beams outside my window, my Hong Kong editor, V. G. Kulkarni, urged me to catch the next flight out, which I did. Once in Hong Kong, I found everyone wearing face masks and gloves, which I quickly donned too. A few days later word got out that the airport might be closed, and I managed to get a ticket on a full flight of escapees from Hong Kong to San Francisco.

Silicon Valley bridge

The importance of being local has been a well-rehearsed industry refrain ever since Benno Schmidt established the first venture capital firm, J.H. Whitney & Co., in 1946. For more than half a century, venture capitalists stayed close to home until suddenly they saw the horizon. Their dreams inflated by the Internet bubble, they began going international, first in the 1990s to the more familiar cultures of Europe and then to Asia around the turn of the century. Many initially looked to English-speaking Singapore as the first stopping-off point in Asia, largely because of that island nation's head-over-heels desire to foster an entrepreneurial climate like that in the Valley. Singapore was a springboard for investments in Southeast Asia. But with the Asian financial crisis of 1997 and the subsequent meltdown of the region's economies, venture capitalists went home empty-handed. China, with its huge markets and newly reforming economy, became the next focal point.

Helping to fuel the increased interest in Chinese start-ups is a reverse migration of U.S.-trained Chinese natives: Stanford- and Berkeley-schooled engineers who were at the front ranks of the Internet revolution. The Chinese government's push to imitate the Valley's tech success in the booming economy is another contributor.

Venture trail

The American venture capital hunters in Beijing and Shanghai have been quick studies in duplicating their Valley formulas in China. First, they commuted to Beijing and Shanghai from San Francisco for a short week of meetings and hurried home for clean air and sunshine. Then they partnered with a strong domestic venture firm in recognition of the need for an on-the-ground presence to find hidden treasures and mitigate the many regulatory and financial risks. The next step was to set up a local office and, in quick succession, raise a China fund.

The final move was to hire Mandarin-speaking locals to do their work and help them pick more than just the low-hanging fruit. The trend became fresh start-ups founded by homegrown Chinese entrepreneurs, many without English-language skills, Western training, or management prowess. Often, equity stakes in those firms could be bought at reduced valuations from what westernized entrepreneurs demanded. That meant higher returns for the venture capitalists when they sold shares.

Breyer of Accel teamed up with IDGVC, an offshoot of the technology publishing and research International Data Group, to raise a $500 million fund in 2007; that was its second China effort after investing at the pace of one deal per month from an initial $310 million joint fund in 2005 with the venture group. David Chao partnered DCM with Legend Capital, an arm of the Chinese conglomerate that owns the Lenovo personal computer business. In early 2006, Chao expanded a Beijing office by recruiting Hurst Lin, former CEO of the large Chinese portal and Nasdaq-listed SINA Corp., as a general partner. Today, DCM has 13 investments in emerging Chinese companies out of a total portfolio of 83 deals in Asia and the United States and has taken several China finds to Nasdaq.

Similarly, the Mayfield Fund started off by partnering with a local player—GSR Ventures in Beijing—before plunging ahead by raising a China fund of $200 million in 2007 with the Chinese firm, whose high-profile partners include James Ding, a cofounder of Nasdaq-listed AsiaInfo in Beijing, and Kevin Fong, an ethnic Chinese venture capitalist with a track record of tech successes in the Valley. Mayfield now has 10 new investments in China. "At some point, we had to stop touring and start investing," Fong says.

The currents became a strong tide as partners defected from U.S. firms to set up their own shops in China. Gary Rieschel, whose wife is Chinese, left Mobius Venture Capital in the Valley to form Qiming Ventures in Shanghai with the Seattle-based Ignition Partners. He's made 14 bets on Chinese innovations since raising $200 million in 2006.

Against that backdrop, domestic venture firms in China sprang into action. One of the first independent Chinese venture firms not connected to a corporate or a local authority was Capital Today Group. It was founded by the former Baring Private Equity Asia managing director Kathy Xu, who raised a $280 million China fund in 2006. Xu and other locals honed in where they felt most comfortable: with the native entrepreneurs, who often were seen as too foreign by the Americans. "The American VCs [venture capitalists] don't speak Mandarin and don't understand the culture," scoffed Xu.

China fever

American venture firms increasingly are closing the gap with their enlightened Chinese strategy of going local. Beware of the stampede. The rush of capital has pushed investment valuations upward and made entrepreneurs stingier about sharing equity in their start-ups with venture financiers. The best entrepreneurs have their pick of venture partners and look for value-added benefits such as knowledge of the local market, networking connections, and experience with recruiting management and going public rather than just cash. Deals that used to be announced with fanfare today remain in "stealth mode," or hidden, to avoid competition.

Striking the right balance of investment in the cyclical venture capital market has many people staying up nights, worrying when and if the fever will break. Len Baker, a managing partner with Sutter Hill Ventures who has honchoed two China deals and advises Chengwei Ventures' managing partner Eric Li in Shanghai, asks, "Ten years from now, will it be great to have moved ahead, or will it be too fast?"

Could the Valley once again be drinking the Kool-Aid, getting a taste of saccharine sweetness from hyped-up claims that provide no energy? Wasn't a lesson learned from the Internet revolution when plenty of Kool-Aid was downed as venture capital money blindly chased deals that later vaporized?

As the decade unfolds, Western venture capitalists will discover how sustainable their China strategies are.

Certainly, China offers far more challenges and risks than does the Sunshine State, and it is still unclear if this surge of investment into China will produce more gems than duds. It takes five years or more to ripen a newly financed start-up for an exit through an acquisition or an IPO. This latest China wave began to swell only in 2005, and so far few fish have been caught. Capital will flow where returns are the greatest and the risks are real but manageable.

The question for venture capitalists and investors is whether China will continue to produce huge growth and the potential for huge profits or whether investors will get tangled in Chinese red tape and a downward economic spiral.

I am betting that a few of the entrepreneurs I've met and interviewed will offer the gold standard of disruptive technology and transform their start-ups into world-class winners. Read the following chapters to meet these innovators, from digital mapmakers to mobile marketers to inventors of a new, efficient light source—all with made-in-China technology. Watch out. The tech leadership race is underway.

part three

THE INNOVATORS

Inspired by Steve Jobs, the purely local hardscrabble team at the Chinese start-up Lingtu creates world-class digital maps of the Middle Kingdom for every imaginable electronic gadget. Having mastered the fine art of digital mapmaking à la Google Earth, it's grooming itself for a public listing.

Lingtu— China's Navigator

The first time I toured Beijing's Forbidden City, in August 1995, it was so hot that I cooled off by drenching myself with bottled water. All the while, I was trailed by a hunched-over peasant who desperately wanted my empty container. I ended up giving it to her so that she would stop following me. She smiled a toothless grin in thanks before hobbling off in the other direction.

Ten years later, conditions for touring the former Imperial Palace are much better, with Beijing a polished, glistening version of its former self. I'm in an air-conditioned conference room, getting an effortless three-dimensional virtual tour by computer monitor of the capital city's top tourist site. Tracking the images on a large screen, I zoom in from a high angle, and get an up-close look at the fine details on the ancient sculptures. The dusty red colors and golden hues are so realistic that it's almost like being there.

Credit for creating this startlingly clear 3-D visual imagery goes to a young company in China called Beijing Lingtu Software Co. It makes a full complement of digital maps for the Internet, CDs, PDAs (personal digital assistants, or computerized handheld personal organizers), mobile phones, cars, and even laptops with built-in Global Positioning Systems.

To the northwest of Beijing, more than an hour's drive from the city center, almost to the mountains and north of the fifth ring road, Lingtu is tucked into the new high-tech hub of Shangdi. Here, the nine-year-old Lingtu (which means "clever maps") is putting itself on the map in rapidly urbanizing China. Four local Chinese techies with not an MBA among them who get their thrills from computerized maps have bootstrapped the operation. Lingtu is not a successful U.S.-style business transplanted to China by a clever Ivy League grad; it is genuinely homegrown Chinese. The firm's key investor, Gobi Partners, named after the nearby desert, is not a Sand Hill Road player but is based in Shanghai. Moreover, Lingtu got its start in 1999, not very long after digital maps first arrived, and the company's skills in the fine art of computerized mapmaking are quite advanced.

The hardscrabble Lingtu team was charging to go public in 2007, but the IPO date has been delayed until 2008 or later. To get pumped up for a public debut, a new CEO and CFO with multinational experience were recruited who can polish up Lingtu's image. Also, the business plan was switched to go after consumer business, where the action is. Such deep fixes even years into a start-up are nothing out of the ordinary for emerging Chinese firms. Most young businesses on the Mainland spring up so quickly that the original business plan and management team have to be scratched. Few businesses are changing as fast as digital mapping. Look at the $8 billion deal Nokia has recently made to acquire the U.S. map and navigational software maker Navteq.

Lingtu's repertoire in China is quite impressive. Besides that 3-D rendering of the Forbidden City, Lingtu has digitally mapped out sites for the Beijing Olympics in 2008 to restrict air pollution, figured out the best spot for a hydroelectric power plant in the Three Gorges dam project, remeasured Mount Everest, pinpointed SARS cases in Beijing during the outbreak of the illness in 2003, and monitored the launch and reentry of China's first manned space flight in that year. A company in the United States would have had to work on the World Trade Center, the Hoover Dam, the Salt Lake City Olympics, the Apollo 11 moon landing, and the peak of Mount McKinley to come close to doing the tasks Lingtu has performed.

Lingtu is unlikely to be a household brand name like the Rand McNally hardcover atlas or even searchable Google Maps on the Web. However, it claims to have the biggest and most comprehensive database of digital maps in the country: some 337 major cities, all 31 provinces, and more than 800,000 kilometers of roads. This is practically 100 percent coverage of urban China. The cities and sites on the maps are all in Mandarin.

Lingtu follows in the navigational wake of the Chinese admirals Zheng He and Wang Jinghong, who, beginning in 1403—years before Columbus—took 62 ships and explored 32 nations, from Persia to East Africa. After seeing and mapping large areas of the globe, the admirals decided they didn't need maps outside China, since the rest of the world was filled with barbarians.

Lingtu's mission of making digital maps in China is no small feat. Consider the fact that about 30 percent of the roads in China change every year. Also, China relies on landmarks, not addresses, for directions. No wonder my taxi drivers are always getting lost! Government licenses are required to enter the digital map business—a high barrier to entry. Lingtu is one of the few private companies with that privilege. Google, for instance, does not have a map-making license in China, though its satellite images of the earth can be seen on the Internet in China, minus views of the Zhongnanhai diplomatic complex where China's leaders live and work and top-secret military compounds.

Then there's the issue of piracy. Lingtu's digital maps are ripped off and sold illegally at a fraction of the original price; that's nothing new to Microsoft or any number of American firms selling in China. Lingtu tackles the issue by cutting counterfeits off from instant map updates. "In China you have to accept that piracy is there. You try to minimize the losses and maximize the upside," says Gobi general partner Lawrence Tse.

Nevertheless, China has one of the fastest-growing digital map markets in the world. What's powering this surge is Global Positioning Systems (GPS), or satellite transmissions to pinpoint locations. Today's China is on the go, using GPS as a guide. The gadget to have is the pricey GPS-tooled smart

> "In China you have to accept that piracy is there. You try to minimize the losses and maximize the upside."
>
> **Lawrence Tse,**
> general partner, Gobi Partners

phone or full-featured computer-like mobile phone that comes with navigation software. A less expensive option is a WAP (wireless application protocol)-enabled mobile phone that has both GPS and Web access to digital maps. GPS also can be found pre-installed or portable in a growing number of privately owned passenger cars. Young and increasingly affluent Chinese consumers would never use printed maps or Yellow Pages directories to find their way.

Map heaven

I arrive at Lingtu in a company car that picked me up so that I wouldn't get lost. The journey takes about an hour in heavy traffic from my comfortable hotel in the new Wall Street-style financial district on the west side. Lingtu has surprisingly contemporary headquarters in a high-tech office park. Entering a spacious marble lobby, I climb the steps, passing a stark white interior courtyard. Upstairs, there's a couple of Ping-Pong tables in a corridor plus a row of carpet samples laid out to select for the next office expansion—both cultural relics of Silicon Valley in the booming late 1990s.

I'm here to interview Lingtu cofounder and former CEO Tang Ningzhe. Tang's assistant, Wenyan Chen, or Anny, a petite young lady whose tight clothes show off her lean frame, leads me into a conference room, leaving me waiting for 10 minutes before Tang bounds in with Anny in tow. Tang, 38 years old, is a round-faced man with uneven teeth, an impatient air, and black hair that sprouts from his head in a bowl-like pattern. He seems nervous, probably because venture partner Tse is supposed to be here. I decide to plunge ahead with my questions, fearing that Tang may have only an hour. I didn't have to worry. We go for two hours before a break for lunch at a restaurant in the complex.

Anny translates for Tang, one of the few Chinese entrepreneurs I've met who doesn't speak English. That doesn't stop him from answering rapid-fire cell phone calls and simultaneously checking his laptop for e-mails as he sketches his biographical details. The firstborn

---

"My dream was to make life more convenient for customers, to make my products and see customers using them. This is exciting."

Tang Ningzhe,
cofounder and chief strategy officer, Lingtu

---

son of engineers, Tang grew up in Hunan province. He was an obedient child but an impatient student who either excelled at or failed in a subject; it all depended on what interested him. Geography is what he liked best and what he was fortunate enough to have an opportunity to pursue.

Tang has devoted his entire life's work and studies to navigation technology in China. He earned an undergraduate degree from Dalian Maritime University in 1994 and then had a job for four years monitoring seagoing vessels for a maritime security unit in Tianjin. Before starting up Lingtu, he was a map technology research fellow at the prestigious Chinese Academy of Science. He credits an inspirational book by Apple Computer founder Steve Jobs that he read in the late 1990s for giving him the entrepreneurial urge. "My dream was to make life more convenient for customers, to make my products and see customers using them," Tang says. "This is exciting."

Knowing his love for maps, I take out my folded paper map of Beijing. He lights up when I ask him to point out where Lingtu is. It turns out it's too far outside central Beijing to be on the map.

Tang brightens as he recalls the early days of Lingtu. It was a tough period but nothing out of the ordinary for any start-up. He and his cofounders practically lived in the office. They went without pay for two months in 2001 when customers didn't pay their bills on time.

As Tang is warming to the topic, venture backer Tse arrives in a rush, unshaved and dressed in jeans, with his briefcase and luggage in tow for a dash to the airport after our meeting. They urge me to view a PowerPoint presentation of the company's mapmaking skills. I take notes madly during the demo as Tse elaborates on the finer details.

Lingtu started out making a few paper maps, but today its entire lineup consists of digital maps of all sorts for a cyber-crazed China. Most of Lingtu's revenues come from the Chinese government and corporations, including Oracle, Hewlett-Packard, and Ericsson, which typically license Lingtu map software for an annual fee. But Lingtu is moving to the dynamic, fast-growth consumer market—a trend for most mapmakers globally.

A CD database of its China maps costs $6. A free map portal called 51ditu.com ("I want maps" in English) offers directions and guides to sights, similar to the familiar Mapquest in the United States, and counts more than 3.5 million users, plus 10,000 Web sites in China that use it as a map interface. Launched in January 2005, 51ditu.com claims to be the first Web site in China to offer ad-supported local search for finding the nearest McDonald's, subway station, or cinema, for example.

What's driving Lingtu is GPS navigation software in cars and on phones. With their product, mobile phone users can, for a small fee, click to find sights and get from point A to point B. Some 10,000 customers get an add-on premium service called CareStar that is handy for monitoring elders or kids who are always wandering off somewhere.

With Lingtu's SmartGPS technology, drivers can get updates on traffic jams or find the nearest gas station. On the corporate front, as many as 40,000 businesses use Lingtu's GPS service to track sales fleets, schedule deliveries, and find the quickest routes. Locating where employees are rather than where they say they are can save a great deal of time and money.

Moving on with the demo, we come to SmartGuider, the sexiest member of the product lineup. To show me how it works, Tse takes out his fully loaded Singapore-made DoPod smartphone—as popular in China as the Blackberry is in the United States—and instantly pulls up a digital map that depicts the roads I took to get to Lingtu's offices, with points of interest such as the Buddhist temple I spotted on a hilltop in the distance. The same technology comes pre-installed on PDAs, including a new Hewlett-Packard PDA model in China. And try to top this: Lingtu claims to have put the first built-in GPS devices in a laptop, a local brand from the Chinese producer Haier. All in all, Lingtu has more than 70 software registrations and copyrights in addition to 17 patents that are pending in China.

What's left for the firm to do in maps? Lingtu wants to integrate the services across mobile phones, the Internet, and CDs and market digital maps on the Web that show landmarks and roadways in three dimensions.

In a world in which making maps has become nearly as high-tech as designing a semiconductor chip and compasses, tape measures, and drafting paper are becoming obsolete, the homegrown Lingtu has developed these map technologies in-house from scratch and excelled. Perhaps this accomplishment should not seem surprising. Years before those Chinese admirals set sail, China developed the compass in the eleventh century, and ancient maps of China depict the Silk Route, the Yellow River, the Great Wall, and the Han Empire's boundaries. The country's advanced surveying technology dates back to the Tang dynasty of the seventh and eighth centuries. China's map-making craftsmen did not fall behind the West until some 40 years ago during the Cultural Revolution even though China was a fairly backward third world nation, suffering famines and civil wars, with little progress from the late nineteenth century until economic reforms began in the late 1970s.

Not everything Lingtu does is so high-tech. To map remote spots in the countryside, for example, Lingtu sends out two-person teams on bikes to record sights with small video cameras. Such a juxtaposition of low tech with high tech would be hard to imagine in the United States, but is not out of the ordinary in the emerging economy of China, where high-speed bullet trains exist side by side with carts pulled by donkeys.

Surveying the market

Computerized maps went commercial in 1985. It is an exacting art; every bridge, tunnel, and bend must be recorded precisely. Today the digital map business is enormous: $60 billion from data, software, and traditional geographic information systems largely for professional logistics use.[1] The wild card is the consumer segment because of the proliferation of mobile phones with GPS receivers.

The Chinese digital map market is soaring as car ownership picks up and mobile phones become as ubiquitous as house keys. By 2012, privately owned vehicles in China with GPS navigational devices will reach almost 25 million, up from nearly 1 million in 2006,[2] and China will narrow the gap between itself and the United States with comparable numbers of 7.2 million in 2006 and 46 million in 2012.[3] Even faster growth is coming for smartphones, PDAs, and cell phones with built-in GPS technology as prices for a standard handset with navigation functions fall from a current $350. By 2012, China will have 19.4 million phones and PDAs with navigation tools, up from 540,000 in 2006, nearly reaching the 2012 U.S. forecast of 23.7 million.[4] Despite these huge growth numbers, the technology may not go mainstream soon. Reading maps on small-screen mobile phones with short battery lives is not for everyone, says analyst Stuart Jeffrey at Lehman Brothers in London.[5]

On a global scale, Lingtu is overshadowed by two large publicly listed mapmakers:[6] Amsterdam-based TeleAtlas and Chicago-based Navteq.[7] Both digital mapmakers entered the Chinese market in recent years, Navteq through a joint venture and TeleAtlas with a licensing agreement.[8] Tiny Lingtu is ramping up quickly in China, its only market so far. Projections for

2007 are at least 30 percent increases over $16 million in revenues and $3 million in profits in 2006.

Lingtu is slugging it out with dozens of start-ups in China. Among them is AutoNavi Software Co., funded by the legendary Sequoia Capital. Some have "killer ap" technology. Three-year-old eDuShi in Hangzhou turns a close-up of a city neighborhood into a 3-D computer-generated map. Shanghai start-up City8.com offers local search with 360-degree panoramic real street scenes, akin to Google's controversial Street View service.[9]

To check out Lingtu more thoroughly, I call Dave Sonnen, a senior consultant at International Data Corp. and a leading digital map expert. He has never heard of the Chinese start-up Lingtu; neither had two other map gurus I tapped in the United States. Sonnen is amazed to find a young Chinese company with such an advanced and comprehensive volume of digital maps. After doing some homework, he concludes that Lingtu has the upper hand over the overseas newcomers because of local industry knowledge and a head start in compiling a large database of China's terrain. "Lingtu's large database and comprehensive map software give it an edge," he says.

"Lingtu's large database and comprehensive map software give it an edge."

Dave Sonnen,
senior consultant, IDC Corp.

Lingtu makes digital maps the Chinese way: quickly and efficiently. For a small company, Lingtu's workforce of 1,000—up from 700 the year before—is huge. Its profit margins of 19 percent are respectable. Low labor costs in China help, but the founding team knows how to stretch a *renminbi* to the nth degree. Consider this: Lingtu has raised $39 million in financing to make digital maps for China, whereas it took TeleAtlas $250 million to enter the U.S. market. "Making maps is a capital-intensive business and takes years to do," venture investor Tse points out. "But Lingtu is able to do this at a much lower rate."

Time for a new CEO

The next time I'm in Beijing, I follow up with Tse to get the latest on Lingtu. Big news awaits me. A new CEO and a new CFO with multinational experience have been hired to supplement the rough-hewn local team, and Tang has become the chief strategy officer. A Stanford grad with U.S. and Asian experience at tech and venture firms, Tse knew such steps were inevitable when he funded Lingtu four years ago.

The two new execs were snatched from the Hong Kong-listed China.com, which parent company CDC Corp. recently downsized and restructured. The new CEO, Albert Lam, was head of China.com for two years and earned managerial stripes from Motorola, Nortel, and General Electric. The new CFO, Vincent Leung, began his career at PriceWaterhouseCoopers and spent two years running CDC's mergers and acquisitions department before working alongside Lam as CFO at China.com. With a road show to prospective investors in the world's financial capitals in the offing, Lingtu needs leaders who know how to talk the talk of Wall Street and look the part. "Because they are expats, they present a better public face to the outside world," says Tse.

The new execs offer a black-and-white contrast to the specialized niche skills of the founding team. Lingtu's head of research and development, Sun Jiang, is former CEO Tang's classmate from the technically oriented Dalian Maritime Institute and has a Ph.D. from the Chinese Academy of Science. The chief technology officer, Sun Yafu, is a former researcher with a national geographic lab and has a master's degree in computer mapping from Wuhan University. The chief software architect, Sun Qingwen, earned an undergraduate degree from and finished some master's studies at the Chinese Academy of Science. Of the four cofounders, Tang is the only one who has traveled to the United States, and that was just once, to Silicon Valley and Seattle on business for Lingtu.

The day after I hear about the management switch, I interview the new CEO, Lam. He outlines his vision of shifting Lingtu to the consumer market. With Chinese ownership of middle- to high-tier phones and passenger cars on the upswing, that's where the growth and the immediate payback are. Lam also is transi-

"Cell phones with built-in GPS will become standard just as camera phones are now the norm."

Albert Lam,
CEO, Lingtu

tioning Lingtu from licensing technology to cell phone and PDA manufacturers to doing paid consumer subscriptions and services. One sure-fire premium service is cell phones with built in software for real-time navigation. "Cell phones with built-in GPS will become standard just as camera phones are now the norm," he predicts.

Meanwhile, Tang diplomatically tells me that he likes his new strategic role because he can "now focus on the crystal ball. By being in charge of business development, I also can work more closely with our important partners." As proof, he points to a recently made deal with a Beijing radio station to offer real-time traffic information to cab drivers.

Back in 2002, Lingtu's young cofounders—all in their late twenties or early thirties—also dealt with top managerial issues. They brought in the seasoned manager Li Zhongliang, age 52, from the state-owned China Construction Bank, gave him a sizable equity stake in Lingtu, and made him chairman. "Here's this young management team. They bring in a gray-haired guy and give him the biggest stake in the company of any individual," recalls Tse. He adds that it's one of the key reasons Gobi made a bet on Lingtu back in 2003. "We were really impressed by their acknowledging that they needed to bring in more talent," he says.

Indeed, Li pulled off a near miracle for Lingtu. During the height of the SARS virus outbreak in mid-2003, he drove 12 hours from Beijing to Shanghai to meet with Tse and his partner, Harvard grad Thomas Tsao. The two partners were holed up in Shanghai, afraid to travel but eager to do a deal with Lingtu. The relentless Li negotiated with the Gobi partners for 11 hours. Meanwhile, as SARS was fading toward the end of the year, Gobi finished raising a $50 million fund to invest in emerging Mainland tech companies. A few months after his trek, Li got a $3 million check from Gobi, the first of the venture firm's nine investments in China.[10] The team compares Li's journey to Chairman Mao's historic Long March from the southeast to the northwest of China

> "Here's this young management team. They bring in a gray-haired guy and give him the biggest stake in the company of any individual."
>
> **Lawrence Tse,**
> general partner, Gobi Partners

during the Chinese Civil War in 1934. "We call it Lingtu's Long Drive," Tse says jokingly.

Lingtu went on to raise $5 million in 2005[11] and $30 million in May 2006.[12] Several would-be investors were turned away.

Photo op

As the PowerPoint presentation winds up during my initial meeting at Lingtu, I take a few photos of Tang in the courtyard as he proudly poses next to a wading pool with goldfish. We head out for lunch past several construction sites before ducking into an empty restaurant. I'm wondering where everyone is. Turns out the employees have lunch in the company canteen. This restaurant is reserved for VIPs.

Tang and his team are proud of their accomplishments and should be. Here's a totally domestic Chinese company toughing it out against multinationals and mastering the fine craftsmanship of producing digital maps. If the new CEO can pump up Lingtu with fatter revenues and profits, the next step will be a public debut at Times Square's Nasdaq. The founders have grown their start-up past adolescence, but reaching maturity is more difficult than they imagined. If Lingtu is successful, this founding team will be able to tell competitors, both domestic and international, where to go and how to get there.

The next company faces some of the same managerial issues. The CEO is the heart and soul of the young company but lacks the deep managerial skills of an executive trained in the West. Yet he somehow has designed a highly innovative mobile service and pulled in large corporate contracts from banks, insurance companies, and brokers. His company is called Oriental Wisdom, which provides some perspective on where this local entrepreneur is coming from.

CHAPTER NINE

Chinese entrepreneur Liu Yingkui has tapped into China's booming mobile phone market and its ferociously capitalist youth by inventing software for selling insurance, mutual funds, and bank accounts—all delivered to a tiny cell phone window. It's a uniquely Chinese idea that combines the best of Verizon and Charles Schwab, and it might become one of China's first tech exports. It all depends on whether Liu can learn to be a manager overnight.

Oriental Wisdom— Confucian Capitalism

Liu Yingkui, who goes by the name "King," has not mastered English yet. That doesn't stop him from hightailing it across town to meet me at my hotel in Beijing and explain, haltingly but passionately, how he spends nearly all his waking hours powering up his Chinese tech company, Beijing Oriental Wisdom Technology Development Co., Ltd. "It is my dream," he says. "I have nothing, only a dream. I forget to sleep, to eat. My dream is my energy."

As this emotionally charged entrepreneur tells me how he works a 16-hour, six-day shift, I am struck by his determination to realize his business vision. Mature for his 31 years, Liu is proud to be Chinese and committed to helping China make a great leap forward through his wits and ability. He is among the first generation of homegrown Chinese entrepreneurs to emerge since the communist nation opened up to capitalism within the last 25 years.

Liu is on to a big future tech trend: marketing, distribution, and customer service—all by mobile phone. This isn't something that might change the world like finding a cure for cancer, but Lingtu is slightly ahead of the big brands Coke, McDonald's, DHL, Microsoft, and Salesforce.com, which have discovered the power of mobile media only in the last few years. The fact that Lingtu was born in the late 1990s and that his company grew out of the young Chinese technician's school project is remarkable.

Unlike many of the clone start-ups described in this book that replicated U.S. businesses, Liu is breaking new ground. His innovative business specializes in the booming financial sector in China.

> "I have nothing, only a dream. I forget to sleep, to eat. My dream is my energy."
>
> **Liu Yingkui,**
> founder and chairman, Oriental Wisdom

For example, its e-magazine, which is designed to be read on a mobile phone, blends financial news blips and quotes from Bloomberg, Morningstar, and Beijing's Shihua Financial Information with ads for Chinese banks, insurance companies, and mutual funds. Liu also wants to distribute financial services to consumers by mobile phone and earn a commission on sales and even help insurers handle claims by cell phone.

"There's no technical barrier now that everyone and his mother is familiar with how SMS [short message service]-based, value-added services work," says Kaiser Kuo, who is group director of digital strategy for the ad agency Ogilvy China in Beijing.

Liu's heroes are not Jobs, Wozniak, and Gates but Liu Bang, who was the first emperor of the Chinese Han dynasty and ruled China from 202 to 195 BC. Abraham Lincoln is another role model. Oriental Wisdom has an entrepreneurial sage as its leader—an individual who is advancing culture by cherishing, respecting, and learning from the past. He is using the advantage of China's millennia of "oriental wisdom" from spiritual and moral leaders ranging from Confucius to Lao Tse to promote his twenty-first-century technology.

Liu tells me that he's pouring his heart into his business not to get rich or famous but out of national pride. With his soulful brown eyes and wrestler's build, Liu has a natural charm that shines through. What Liu is determined to prove with Oriental Wisdom is that China can make a great leap forward in this new era of digitalization.

Right product, right market

Oriental Wisdom's timing is impeccable. The country's burgeoning financial markets are undergoing a rapid transformation from state control to private ownership, and foreign banks are boosting competition as they go into China under terms set by that nation's entry into the World Trade Organization in 2001. Thrifty Chinese consumers are known for saving and for gambling. They are increasingly sophisticated about options for getting better investment returns from their hard-earned savings rather than using the old "stuff it under the mattress" technique or hoping for a lucky streak at a casino in Macau off the southern coast of Mainland China. Investing in the stock market by ordinary Chinese citizens, even taxi drivers, is common.

Combine that trend with China's huge mobile phone market, and you have two big drivers for Oriental Wisdom. Unlike the United States, in China consumers never got used to the laptop personal computer or the PDA personal organizer. China jumped right into cell phones, which far outnumber traditional landline phones. Mobile phones are not just for chatting but provide a powerful new media channel. Radio, television, and newspapers can't compare to the personal, handy, convenient cell phone. Some people even keep their mobiles switched on all night by the bedside.

Forget the old 30-second television commercial. Armed with software and a database of customer contacts and purchasing habits, marketers are aiming text and multimedia ads directly at a customer's cell phone. That's far more efficient than forcing products on unresponsive consumers.

No wonder worldwide ad spending on mobile phones is projected to rise to $11.4 billion in 2011 from $1.5 billion in 2007.[1] The Chinese mobile ad market, fueled by steady economic growth and the upcoming Beijing Olympics, is set to leap to $350 million by 2011 from approximately $60 million in 2007 and climb to about $100 million in the 2008 Olympic year.[2] Mobile advertising is commanding a greater proportion of total marketing budgets in China too.[3]

Shopping on the mobile Internet for everything from movie tickets to subway rides also is catching on and someday may replace the use of credit cards and cash. Revenues from so-called m-commerce will reach $40 billion by 2009.[4] Boosted by sales of mobile games, ringtones, and dating services, Chinese m-commerce is growing by nearly 20 percent annually.[5]

China is the Promised Land. Super-speedy third-generation (3G) wireless technology is coming soon as the government pushes to transform China into a world-class mobile leader like South Korea and Japan.[6] The much-anticipated service is predicted to be ready by the Beijing Olympics in summer 2008. When that happens, China's mobile phone users will be streaming video, viewing ads, buying services, playing multimedia games, and downloading music like there's no tomorrow. Already loads of Chinese financial services are shooting ads and services directly to customers' cell phones.

Tiny Oriental Wisdom has carved out a big chunk of the Chinese financial services market as clients: 3 of the nation's largest insurance companies—China Life, Pacific Insurance, and New China Life—plus 14 others, in addition to 3 banks and 48 mutual fund companies. It even counts a Chinese offshoot of the U.S. investment firm Franklin Templeton as a client. Oriental Wisdom lures them with a package of ads sprinkled with quick news tidbits on the stock market, real estate, and the economy.

Chinese citizens who grew up in the country's state-owned economy never had the "luxury" of receiving a cold call from an overly eager insurance agent promising the moon with a new savings account or life insurance policy. Now Oriental Wisdom is consigning to history the beleaguered insurance salesperson who withstands slammed doors and threatening dogs in the yard. With Oriental Wisdom, a cell phone is better than a foot in the door as a method of selling.

The seven-year-old Oriental Wisdom is small but has a first-mover advantage and market leadership in a specialized niche. The company had $3.2 million in revenues and $60,000 in profits for 2006. The goal for 2007 was $7.4 million in revenues and $252,000 in profits, climbing to $20 million in revenues and $3.3 million in profits in 2008.[7] Lingtu has a staff of 180 employees but needs capital to grow. Fund-raising is under way after the collection of $8 million two years ago from Tina Ju of TDF Capital and Kleiner Perkins and Jenny Lee of Granite Global Ventures in Shanghai. CEO Liu is lucky to have these detail-oriented and strategic venture capitalists on his board of directors; this is probably the only Chinese tech start-up with two female board members in the clubby male venture space.

With a charismatic leader like Liu who has such good instincts, what could go wrong? For starters, Oriental Wisdom is in a hot area that is bound to become crowded with competitors. Already, rivals have lined up: the large

Chinese Internet portal SINA and the software firm Neusoft in addition to the telecom operators China Unicom and China Telecom, which have rolled out popular mobile phones with pre-installed stock and financial services software. Additionally, Oriental Wisdom needs more capital to get into the direct distribution of financial services by mobile phone. Liu started tapping the money well in spring 2007.

Oriental Wisdom has to keep inventing marketing gimmicks such as free currency converters, risk calculators, and portfolio management tools to entice the right consumers.[8] The majority of Chinese mobile subscribers are low-end users, not likely buyers of financial services. To be successful, Oriental Wisdom must "build its brand to high-end users and partner with reliable financial and insurance companies," says Duncan Clark of BDA Consulting in Beijing.

Management hurdles

The biggest issue for Oriental Wisdom is management. Liu, like many other young, passionate entrepreneurs, wants to try a lot of new things without real grounding. This is his first stab at entrepreneurship, and his board keeps reining him in. For instance, he's had to drop two areas beyond the firm's core competency: mobile games and software training for building features on mobile phones. But he has the risk-taking DNA of a successful entrepreneur.

Liu is representative of the new breed of innovator in today's China; he has honed his technological abilities entirely on the Mainland, not in one of America's finer institutions of learning. His three cofounders are all locals too. The chief financial officer, Bill Huang, and the head of marketing, Kevin Cheng, joined the start-up from a venture capital firm Liu was pitching for money to form Oriental Wisdom. The technology chief, Steven Fu, is a former classmate of Liu's and has a Ph.D. in computer science. Workaholic that he is, Liu can't make up for a lack of managerial experience and Silicon Valley know-how—that is understandable in light of the fact that capitalism is a new force in China. Venture investor Tina Ju says that Liu may have to accept working alongside a more seasoned executive to help the young company mature.

That advice may be hard for Liu to digest. He is a natural competitor who keeps himself in shape by swimming nearly every morning before he drives to the office. Though he lives at home with his parents and his mother still takes care of some chores for him, including packing his lunch, there's no denying his leadership skills—from young political leader in his hometown to university class president.

Investor partner Ju remembers meeting Liu for the first time. "I was impressed by his vision and his maturity for his young age. I listened to his background—it was quite impressive and interesting," she says. "These were a lot of accomplishments for such a young age. There was something special about him too to have these capabilities. For someone to have such a strong grasp of politics as well as business—I felt he almost has it all: people skills, business sense, and leadership," says Ju, who is a good judge of character.[9]

> "I was impressed by his vision and his maturity for his young age."
>
> **Tina Ju,**
> managing partner,
> KPCB China and TDF Capital

Her words "almost has it all" have less to do with the person than with his ability to implement and execute a bold strategy. Indeed, Oriental Wisdom has a tall order to fill. "The business model he is building is extremely ambitious. He is trying to change the way financial products will be distributed in the long run," she observes.

Meeting Mr. Wisdom

The next time I'm in Beijing, I arrange to meet Liu at his office in Tower A in a modern office complex across the freeway from Beijing's rising Olympic Village. The young company's headquarters are plush with all-white walls, glassed-in office suites, and leather couches. When I remark on the decor, Liu explains that he needs the luxurious surroundings because he's dealing with clients in the financial business. "I don't want an office so big," he says, "but our customers are financial advisers, so we must pay attention to image. It is financial IT [information technology] work we are doing, not just IT work," he points out.

It becomes clear to me that Liu doesn't care much about high-priced trappings when I spot some framed calligraphy hanging on a wall in his office.

I ask Liu to translate the Chinese characters. "It doesn't matter what the place is, it matters who is in the place," he reads, explaining that the phrase comes from an ancient Chinese emperor.

Liu was born in the thriving industrial city of Harbin in northeastern China, a region once under Russian rule. His father often would come home from his job as an engineer in one of the city's many plants and tutor young Liu in Chinese history. That made a lasting impression. "The history of China influenced me very much. I feel I must do something to change society, to push society to upgrade," he says. "I like my country very much," he continues, choosing the English words carefully to convey his meaning in a language he doesn't speak well. "I want to do something for my dream, for my China."

He adds that his dream is to create a successful Chinese enterprise that can "face the world" and be known internationally. "I want to say that this business from China can work and that it works because it is from China," he sums up. I haven't had a discussion with any entrepreneur in my 15-plus years covering international business who remotely compares to Liu's philosophical bent.

"I want to say that this business from China can work and that it works because it is from China."

Liu Yingkui,
founder and chairman, Oriental Wisdom

Liu graduated from Northeastern University, a large institute known primarily for its engineering school, in the industrial city of Shenyang in northeastern China. He aced the school's bachelor's and master's programs in computer science. His life-changing moment came when his class software project won first prize in a nationwide computer science contest. That work became the basis for Oriental Wisdom in 2000.

This isn't rocket science. Oriental Wisdom bases its software code on a wireless technology called BREW (Binary Runtime Environment for Wireless) developed by the San Diego firm Qualcomm. BREW is a platform for mobile services that range from downloading ringtones to playing games to recognizing speech patterns.[10] Oriental Wisdom is one of 600 companies in China that use this technology and has been given an award for effectiveness and innovation by Qualcomm.

Milestones pile up

Liu's business concept and technology were too advanced for the market when he introduced them to China early in this decade. "We had to put our heart down and wait for the market to grow up," he says. Times were so rough that the cofounders couldn't buy food or pay the rent. The apartment they were living in, courtesy of a friend, caught fire. They all escaped without harm, an experience that cemented a strong bond among the founders.

Oriental Wisdom got its first big breakthrough four years ago: a contract from the large insurer China Life. "In 2003, our company is very small, and providing a big service for this customer is a very big challenge for us," Liu says.

Today Oriental Wisdom sells to about 80 percent of China's insurers and 90 percent of its mutual fund firms. About two-thirds of revenues come from a mobile customer service package that lets on-the-go salespeople access a database of users and, with analytical tools, track sales patterns with data linked to headquarters. The sales reps can see, for instance, if a message has been received, has bounced back, or has not been answered. Mobile marketing promotions account for about 15 percent of revenues, with the remainder coming from software licenses.

Oriental Wisdom's ad rates are a bargain. To reach 1,000 customers, it charges $5 for a text message and $21 for a multimedia version, compared with an average cost of $500 to reach 1,000 customers in the United States through a highly targeted Internet ad campaign.

Oriental Wisdom's ad package of eight financial news items blended in with one promotional message verges on being an intrusive advertorial. However, investor Ju argues that the sparing use of ads is "really not that invasive."

The company's miniature e-magazine, which is viewed through a simplified Internet browser designed for mobile phones, offers a soft sell approach that pulls in consumers with highly customized financial news and advertorials sent to 7 million VIP customers. Content is displayed in high-color resolution on the phone's tiny screens. The e-zine seeks to boost consumer loyalty and trust by avoiding 'in your face" useless investment pitches.

Next, Oriental Wisdom wants to rent its comprehensive database of 12 million financial service customers—including demographic profiles and customer phone numbers—to advertisers. It needs the customers' permission first. Most financial institutions in China don't have their own sales databases.

Over coffee with investor Tina Ju at Shanghai's Marriott Hotel, a popular place with expatriate business executives, she tells me how she was won over by Liu. The apartment fire survival tale did it. "I was immediately persuaded that this was a team I could back," she says. Before she went with her instincts, her team checked out Liu's company thoroughly and talked to his customers. During the due diligence, Liu signed up three of the six biggest insurance companies in China. In 2004, Venture TDF—Ju's first venture stop— invested a small sum in Oriental Wisdom. "I was pretty impressed with his ability to sign contracts at large institutions," she says.

> *"King is dealing with very large companies, and they have high expectations. He promises a lot, and they think, 'Great, but can he help us launch a nationwide campaign?'"*
>
> **Tina Ju,**
> managing partner,
> KPCB China and TDF Capital

In any fast-growing business, the challenge is to deliver on promised services once contracts have been signed. "King is dealing with very large companies, and they have high expectations. He promises a lot, and they think, 'Great, but can he help us launch a nationwide campaign? Can we get all the insurance agents in the organizations to sign in?' That becomes a huge challenge for a small company like Oriental Wisdom," she says.

Liu has a tendency to drive his people very hard, Ju says. She tells me how Liu makes his salespeople copy the material in the firm's 300-page training manual so that they will learn and remember it.

But high energy and commitment can't substitute for managerial finesse. She confides, "At some point, we do need to help him find a very capable COO and expand the company a little more aggressively." She notes that Liu recognizes the importance of building the best team. "Each time we see him at a board meeting, we try to preach to him about recruiting the best team members. He is gradually doing that and is much more open to that," she says. "He has done an excellent job of recruiting dedicated and capable engineers."

Any entrepreneur with venture capitalists in tow must learn to deal with such flash points and let go. One major concession he's made is giving outside investors a 50 percent ownership stake in his start-up. The shares went to Venture TDF and TDF Capital, as well as to Granite Global Ventures, which invested $8 million in August 2005. Such a large holding by outside investors is almost unheard of in the West; but a clause in the contract allows the founding team to gain a larger stake if certain financial goals are met.

"At some point, we do need to help him find a very capable COO and expand the company a little more aggressively."

Tina Ju,
managing partner,
KPCB China and TDF Capital

How the shares will be divvied up as Oriental Wisdom prepares to raise more capital is uncertain. Getting the right mix is likely to be a tension point in contract talks. It's only human to expect a financial reward for so much challenging and pioneering work, but the team must balance a need for capital against ambition to benefit from the results of its labor. That, of course, is the dilemma of any start-up.

As it is, Oriental Wisdom is balancing Chinese traditions and thought with current global business practices. There's no mention of going public yet. The young firm has got to break out of "smalldom." The management issue must be resolved amicably too. But Oriental Wisdom has several favorable attributes: a highly dedicated, fully charged CEO with a mighty heart, plus the huge market opportunity in financial services and mobile marketing. Silicon Valley startups should be so lucky. Now Liu must turn Oriental Wisdom into a moneymaking machine. After all, he does not want to let down his investors or, for that matter, his country.

The next innovative Chinese entrepreneur I profile is a toned-down version of Liu, also a native Chinese with no work or education experience outside his homeland. Nonetheless, he has taken the bold step of creating a new technology for China that is beginning to catch on globally. His software is based on the ubiquitous cell phone—a way to keep the world connected wirelessly with mobile text messaging anywhere, anytime, for free. What could be better?

Move over, Skype. Here comes PingCo, which brings chatting, dating, and game playing to the mobile phone in a David-versus-Goliath battle with China's Ma Bell. CEO Charles Wang has made PingCo such a phenomenon that "ping me" now means "send me a message" in a country where the mobile Internet is as cool as Hotmail once was in the United States.

PingCo— Ping Me, Please

In Beijing, sending short messages by mobile phone is an addiction. I join in with my own Chinese mobile phone and prepaid service card. Getting set up takes an afternoon with the help of my Beijing office assistant, Summer. We go to a nearby electronics store, Gome, a dusty, tired-looking version of Circuit City. Inside, several counters of cheap-looking Chinese phones are on display under dim fluorescent lights. I pass them up in favor of a sleek Nokia model made in China. I head for one of the cheerless clerks standing behind the glass counters. There's not one customer in sight; it should be a breeze.

An hour of behind-the-scenes paperwork later, I pay for it with my MasterCard and obtain an official government-stamped receipt. My new Nokia doesn't come cheap at $155. How can a Beijing worker with an average salary of about $500 a month afford a decent cell phone? That's easy. Toting the latest and niftiest mobile phone is a much bigger deal than owning a car, a laptop, or a TV.

The next stop is a branch of the state-owned phone network China Mobile to sign up for service. Here the line is about 20 people deep. I take a number and wait to be called. When my turn finally comes, Summer helps me order a card that is valid for three months and up to three hours of talk time, all for $8. I insert my handy SIM (subscriber identity module) card, or smartcard, that will function as the brains of my Nokia. Now I can make calls locally in China and avoid roaming charges for international long distance on the mobile phone I use in the United States. Great: Now I can do what the locals do.

The next morning I'm off to meet a local Bloomberg news correspondent for lunch. I have my Nokia in hand when she sends me a short-text message. She's running late. Not used to the miniature English-letter keyboard, I simply type "OK." Soon every contact I have in Beijing wants to SMS me. So much for e-mail or voice mail, which still are more popular than SMS in the United States.

Text messaging is all the rage. In China, credit goes in part to a two-year-old mobile Internet service called PingCo that was invented by Chinese entrepreneur Charles Wang. Using PingCo, you can send free messages with no limits, assuming that the monster phone operator China Mobile doesn't put it out of business. If PingCo perseveres against that giant near monopoly, it promises to be as popular as the Apple iPhone or Skype, an overnight international sensation with its free chat and text service over the Web in real time. PingCo is the mobile version of Skype, one of the world's first free Web 2.0 services over mobile phones, followed only by a handful of similar start-ups worldwide. CEO Wang is ahead of the trends with his new invention. It helps that he worked for two American companies in China.

PingCo, which is shorthand for Personal Information Next Generation, or "ping," as in "ping me" ("send me a message"), promises to be a killer application for wireless communications. It could be the next new thing that feeds consumers' appetite for more. It also breeds addictive behavior.

PingCo is not just text messages but also mobile chat, games, and matchmaking. Many of the basic services are free now, but PingCo is beginning to charge for premium add-ons such as a next-generation dating service that lets potential mates talk online before committing to a night out. Want to read an e-book on a mobile phone? PingCo offers that too. For a monthly charge of $1.30 or 2 cents per 1,000 words, subscribers can flip digitally through the pages of thousands of e-books from the Chinese e-book publisher www.17k.com. How about playing a game online with a friend? For less than a penny, players can buy virtual weapons to do battle. PingCo has developed all these unique-to-China services, with the exception of the books and complex games, on its own.

"We thought that if we could take the most popular Internet services on the personal computer—chatting, dating, and video downloads—and bring them to the mobile phone, we would have a killer ap," says PingCo CEO Wang, using American tech slang for a hot new feature.

For billing, PingCo uses a virtual currency cleverly denominated in digital apples, a favored food of its mascot and logo, a prickly but playful hedgehog.

PingCo has leapfrogged past the current rage of blogs and video downloads on the Net and gone straight to the mobile Web 2.0 and always-on portable entertainment. "The mobile Internet is to the PC-based Internet what television was to radio," says Alan Moore, a high-tech consultant at Engagement Marketing in Cambridge, United Kingdom.

"We thought if we could take the most popular Internet services on the personal computer—chatting, dating, and video downloads—and bring them to the mobile phone, we would have a killer ap."

Charles Wang,
CEO, PingCo

The start-up's original, made-in-China technology is geared to capitalize on the Mainland's gigantic mobile phone market. China leads the world in instant messaging,[1] and youngsters here can't wait to hook up wirelessly. Text messaging by phone is more popular than e-mail, voice mail, or even television and music. Some 126 million people use instant messaging: more than two-thirds of the "netizens" in the country. Many have more than one account.[2] College students in Beijing and Shanghai send an average of 1,000 SMSs per month, or about 33 per day, spending more than $15 monthly for their text message service (SMS) habit.

For drama, you can't beat the classic David-versus-Goliath battle of PingCo against state-owned China Mobile.[3] PingCo is one of the first Chinese companies to circumvent that near monopoly, and it's taking a bite out of the profits the giant mobile phone network makes from text messaging and mobile 2.0 services. "We don't want to be too close to the phone carriers," Wang says. "It is better to be independent and focus on value for the users."

PingCo is rooted in China, from its well-grounded founder to its investor, GSR Ventures, down the road from the start-up's office in Beijing's high-tech zone. PingCo is not making money yet, but Wang says that his start-up will break even in 2007 on $1.5 million in revenues. Wang has raised a solid $8.5 million from investors, and his goal is to take PingCo public in two or three years. Revenues, which are climbing steadily, come from new premium offerings, including a popular program that lets people log on to PingCo to vote for "superboy" in a TV show similar to *American Idol*. Also boosting the bottom line are mobile service advertisers for dating, commerce, and e-learning. Kodak and Cisco are in the wings as prospective marketers.

> "The only thing holding PingCo back from becoming another Skype is awareness; that's it."
>
> **Kevin Fong,**
> managing director, Mayfield Fund

If China Mobile doesn't do PingCo in—and that's a big if—PingCo could be another Hotmail, the Web-based e-mail service that debuted in 1996 and in little more than year had nearly 8.5 million users including grandmas who discovered the joys of sending e-mails to friends. Within two years of its start date in May 2005, PingCo signed up 7 million users, with 10 million in sight by the end of 2007.

The fact that a finely tuned consumer creation like this sprung out of newly reforming China is exceptional. China has come a long way from the earlier era of copycat entrepreneurs who took ideas from the West and brought them home on a high-tech Silk Road. But history has come full circle: A thousand years ago, China was far more advanced than Europe and it was Europeans doing the copying.

The experienced tech investor Kevin Fong, a managing director at Mayfield Fund in Silicon Valley, made sure PingCo was one of his firm's first Chinese investments. "The only thing holding PingCo back from becoming another Skype is awareness; that's it," Fong says.

Meeting Mr. PingCo

Wang picks me up in his light blue late-model BMW. My early-morning meeting was at his investor GSR's office, overlooking the new headquarters for Google China across the street. We are only a few blocks from Wang's alma mater, Tsinghua University. Giving me a toothy grin, Wang offers to drive by the school. At the university gates he pulls the car over and pauses to let me snap several pictures of him posing with his snazzy car and its license plate with many 9's, Wang's lucky number. Bright, young, earnest-looking graduate on his way up in the world—it's not a bad image. But from Wang's reserved demeanor, you'd never know it.

As China opens to the world, Charles Wang is only one among a large talent pool of young and motivated engineers showing Silicon Valley their stuff. Expect a lot more tech whizzes to turn up, emerging from China's switched-on entrepreneurial zones and inventing new technology—and in the thick of the hot mobile Internet area, like PingCo. Having grown up poor during the Cultural Revolution, many Chinese entrepreneurs—Wang included—are used to working hard and are not afraid to fail. Indoctrinated in the communist philosophy of a harmonious society, they are working for a better tomorrow and emerging as a quiet but powerful force today in Chinese society and tomorrow perhaps all over the world.

Wang, who is 33 years old, was born in a small town outside Hangzhou in the flourishing private enterprise province of Zhejiang in eastern China. His schoolteacher parents encouraged him to seek new horizons. Wang left home for Beijing and graduated from Tsinghua in 1996 with a bachelor's degree in electrical engineering. He then joined Hewlett-Packard (HP) as a corporate trainee in Beijing. His rare-in-China multinational experience served him well. Thanks to a strong bond with his mentor, HP's Chinese manager Ricky Lee, Wang's career took off. Within two years, he was promoted to sales manager at HP.

In 1999, when Lee left HP for a state-owned information technology enterprise called Founder Group, Wang joined him to help initiate reforms at the money-losing company. At age 26, he was put in charge of a joint venture between Founder and Yahoo! to handle ad sales for the U.S. Internet portal's Mandarin-language site. In 2001, the venture was spun off as a Hong Kong public company with Founder and Yahoo! as the controlling shareholders. But by 2003, the Internet bubble had burst, and the Yahoo! venture was struggling to keep up with Chinese portals that had more local content than Yahoo!'s translated content from the United States. Wang's mentor Lee, meanwhile, set off to start a software firm in Shanghai and asked Wang to join him.

But that time his young protégé opted to strike out on his own. "You can't always follow the mentor," says Wang. "It was time for me to do something by myself."

Wang worked as a sales director for two years in Beijing for the French smartcard chip maker Gemplus. He bumped into Tiger Wu, a programmer who developed SMS software for China Mobile. Wu was a 1996 graduate of Beijing Union University and a software coding genius. They teamed up to start PingCo, betting on the fast-growing market for mobile Internet services.

"PingCo is pursuing a calculated but risky path. What it is doing is not illegal. But China Mobile could put any company out of business."

Kevin Fong,
managing director, Mayfield Fund

As a safety net, Wang's wife, a classmate from university days, kept her job as an information technology manager at the formerly state-owned and now Hong Kong-listed China Merchant Bank. The young couple lives in the countryside near the mountains surrounding Beijing, where Wang's mother looks after their three-year-old son. "My wife wanted to keep her job. We didn't want to put all our eggs in one basket," says Wang, using an American colloquialism that sometimes is heard these days in urban China.

This is Wang's first start-up, and most new businesses fail. Still unprofitable and dependent on venture capitalists, PingCo has to show traction with advertisers and consumers and monetize its services, says Duncan Clark of the advisory firm BDA. But PingCo is in the right line of work. "We believe instant messaging is a good community platform, both online and wireless," Clark says, "which can keep users coming back for more."

Clark points out that PingCo now has competition in China from players with similar services. Microsoft's MSN and Tencent's QQ offer mobile instant messaging for a fee. Additionally, the newcomer PICA has attracted more than 6 million users to a free Web-based instant messaging service for mobile phones. For about 70 cents a month, PICA customers also can blog, read news, search, and read electronic books.

Technology aside, there is a whopper of a difference between PingCo and the rest of the crowd: It's the only one going up against China Mobile, the huge cell phone operator with 300 million customers. What would happen if China Mobile went after little PingCo? We may find out soon. In June 2007, China Mobile launched its own free mobile messaging service, Fetion, with a goal of attracting 25 million individual accounts.[4]

"China Mobile doesn't know if PingCo is a good thing or a bad thing."

Charles Wang,
CEO, PingCo

Each time Chinese consumers buy a service over a mobile phone in China, the mobile operator takes about a 40 percent cut of revenues from the content provider. By skirting the Ma Bells of China, PingCo's free service takes a slice of revenues and profits from the operator. But PingCo users must subscribe to the mobile operator's data service package, which costs about $2.50 monthly, for text messaging. "China Mobile doesn't know if PingCo is a good thing or a bad thing," says Wang. "And they know they can't block us without blocking all China Mobile's users."

China Mobile still might unleash an all-out assault on its upstart rival. "PingCo is pursuing a calculated but risky path," says Mayfield director Fong. "What it is doing is not illegal. But China Mobile could put any company out of business."

The SMS world is flat

Globally, this free mobile SMS sector is one to watch. A handful of similar services emerged in early 2006, about half a year after PingCo's debut. In a sign that technology trends travel worldwide, the start-ups come from everywhere: Rebtel Networks in Stockholm, NimBuzz in the Netherlands, Crickee in Paris, Hotxt in the United Kingdom, and Jajah in Mountain View, California, and Ra'anana, in a suburb of Tel Aviv.

None of them has entered China. PingCo stands a good chance of becoming much larger in its local market than any of those look-alike services. Phones with GPRS—the kind that can run PingCo's features—are being adopted quickly in China as well as in the rest of Asia and in Europe. Currently, only 8 percent of mobile phones in China have GPRS technology, but Wang predicts that by 2008, nearly 90 percent of phone purchasers will upgrade to models with GPRS.

Against the noise of rivals, PingCo is ramping up very fast. PingCo raised $3 million from GSR and Mayfield in August 2005, when the company was only three months old. PingCo soon hired 10 employees.[5] Today, it has 60. In June 2007, PingCo got what every young company needs: an additional $5.5 million from investors.[6]

Alex Pan, a managing director at GSR, tells me that his team had some initial reservations about funding PingCo because it was new and untried. But the venture partners were won over after seeing a prototype of the service. It was the type of disruptive technology service they were searching for, the kind that can result in a financial home run. PingCo software runs on Java, the same platform used by developers to design mobile games. Today, PingCo is one of the more promising finds among the 14 start-ups GSR has supported since mid-2005.

Tsinghua sightlines

Back with Wang in his BMW, we drive along the wide boulevards of this new tech zone in Beijing and pull into the garage of his office building. It's a state-owned building that houses the government's bureau for registering new businesses. Wang has managed to get a bargain rental rate here. His corner office has a view of the Tsinghua campus.

Wang sets aside the morning for our interview. He patiently and methodically goes over the business plan as staff people keep interrupting with questions. Wang is not distracted by them or by the text messages he continually receives. He pauses to show me how to check how many minutes I have left on my China Mobile phone card. It turns out there's an English version of the prompts to follow, so it's pretty simple.

Knowing that my interview is his chance for Western press that might give PingCo a push to an initial public offering (IPO), Wang focuses on the key issue: how PingCo is going to make money. Wang intends to get subscribers hooked on the basic text messaging service and then sign them up for paid premium services such as backing up address books online, astrology charts, and weather updates. Then he plans to get advertising revenues from marketers who want to reach PingCo customers: Most are males between the ages of 18 and 25, but with a monthly income of only $266. That could be a hard sell.

One plus is that PingCo can target ads to specific groups of subscribers. PingCo's nifty software analyzes messages for keywords in the content. Then PingCo pushes ads to users that match their interests according to the keywords (this is similar to the methodology used by Google's AdSense program). If a subscriber makes a purchase from the advertisers, PingCo splits the revenue with the promoter.

Say I want to find a place to stay on Hainan Island, the new Hawaii-like resort area in southern China. The word *resort* is picked up as a keyword in my message to a friend. Then my cell phone number is turned over to a marketer pushing travel promotions to that destination.

This strikes me as an invasion of privacy. But Wang emphasizes that PingCo gets permission from subscribers, winning them over with small incentives such as free access to mobile games before turning over their phone numbers to marketers. For every name PingCo recruits, it receives 25 cents from the marketer. Internet users have accepted online ads, but wouldn't unsolicited ads be a major nuisance on cell phones? Still, free SMS is cool enough that young Chinese don't much care.

How long before free SMS and the mobile Internet take off in the United States? Perhaps not too long, judging from the way innovation is being sparked from the most unexpected sources and traveling across time zones. PingCo doesn't have plans to go global, but it could someday. If PingCo can continue to one-up China Mobile, it will be because it has some winning attributes: good leadership, innovative service, and great timing.

Our next entrepreneur has his own leading-edge technology: a new browser for the Web that makes Internet Explorer look dated. And talk about lucky: This software developer was mentored by the guy who unearthed Skype and has the blessing of a whole community of software developers who are working with him for free. Plus, he has a huge fan club of more than 100 million users worldwide who love his software. It is the first Chinese technology to break through the country's borders and register globally.

CHAPTER ELEVEN

Jeff Chen developed a Chinese Internet browser that makes surfing the Web as easy as changing television channels by remote control. Even Microsoft has adopted some of its features. With a famous Scandinavian mentor to guide him, could Chen and Maxthon be in Google's crosshairs?

Maxthon—
The Way China Surfs
the World

At the Kerry Centre Hotel in central Beijing in April 2005, the ballroom is filled with investors attending the annual Asian Technology Roundtable Exhibition. They're here to spot the next wave of promising private technology companies in Asia. Software developer Jeff Chen is presenting to a group eager to find uncut diamonds that can be turned into sparkling assets. As geeky as Bill Gates ever was, Chen doesn't have much stage presence. His mentor Morten Lund, the Copenhagen investor who put Skype into orbit, had to coax Chen to pitch for funding here. Lund even prepared the PowerPoint slides for him.

Chen ticks off the functions on his highly customizable browser: open multiple Web pages by using tabs; perform commands such as "go back," "go forward," and "refresh" with tiny gestures on the mouse; capture and save Web pages as files; block ads; zoom in on pages; and boost speeds for downloads. My personal favorite is an undo command to go back to a page that was closed accidentally. Microsoft didn't come out with similar features for its Internet Explorer Version 7 until a year and a half later, in fall 2006.

As he leaves the stage, investors crowd around Chen. He is the man of the hour. A mechanical engineer by training who plays computer games in his downtime, Chen finds the attention overwhelming. "This is my first public speech. I don't think my speech is very good," he says.

In the corridor, beefy-looking and outgoing Peter Liu of the U.S.-Chinese venture firm WI Harper corners Chen. "You're mine. Let's go to dinner," he tells the young software developer known in cyberspace by his code name, BloodChen. Over a dinner that evening with the VIPs who attended the show, Lund whispers in Liu's ear. He explains how during a trip to Israel in 2004 he discovered a bunch of hard-core techies using the Chinese browser, which was called MyIE2 at that time. He tried it out and fell in love with the ability of the rich set of customizable features to improve surfing online. He spent three months sending instant messages to Chen before he got on a plane from Denmark to meet the Chinese software developer. Lund offered Chen what every budding entrepreneur wants: a check (for $120,000) and help in building the start-up. Everyone got pretty drunk at the dinner in Beijing, but the next morning Lund and Chen made a handshake deal with Liu for WI Harper to invest $500,000.

Chen says of his mentor, "He can sell anything."

It was actually a fairly easy sale. Chen had developed a breakthrough browser. Only one other browser in the market—Firefox—made surfing the Web so easy and enjoyable, and Chen's browser predated Firebox by about a year. Working mostly in China, Chen had done it pretty much on his own with support from a community of software developers for tests and debugs of the program.

"This is my first public speech. I don't think my speech is very good."

Jeff Chen,
founder and CEO, Maxthon

"You're mine. Let's go to dinner."

Peter Liu,
chairman, WI Harper

At the conference was an influential fan of Chen's: Kaiser Kuo, then *Red Herring*'s China bureau chief. Kuo took his friend, American tech investor Bill Tai, aside and clued him in on the innovative browser. Before long Tai and Chen were enjoying a relaxing Chinese foot massage at a local spa and talking nonstop about Web soft-

ware. On the spot, Tai told Chen that he would fund the Chinese firm. With the deal in the works, Tai raced to the airport and just made his flight. His seat number was 88A—8's symbolize wealth in Chinese culture. Tai used his camera phone to snap his own photo holding up the boarding pass. "I knew right then and there this was good luck. We had good chemistry, and this deal[1] was going to work," Tai said.

The deal showcased the impressive technology coming today from China and the gold rush to make money from a new Silicon Valley on the other side of the Pacific.

Chen's start-up, Maxthon, produces a made-in-China browser that improves surfing on the Net in a communist country that censors content on the Web. Its surf-friendly features surely will have a positive impact on Chinese society. Think of all those teens in Beijing and Shanghai Internet cafés. It was satellite television beamed from Hong Kong into Mainland China that first gave the Chinese a view of the Western world. Now the Web offers nearly infinite possibilities for seeing the world. A better browser is a key to the enormous resources on the Web for businesses and consumers alike.

Maxed out

Maxthon is one of the first Chinese tech inventions to go global. About one-third of its users live in the United States and Europe. Maxthon is available in 20 languages, including English; not bad compared with Internet Explorer, which is available in 25 languages. But its backbone is Chinese. Maxthon's development team and most of its partners are in China. Some features, though not specifically designed for locals, appeal to Chinese users. They include a built-in ad blocker that gets rid of the seemingly endless ads that pop up on Chinese-language Web pages and so-called proxy support to access Web pages anonymously and bypass blocked sites.

Word of Maxthon has spread quickly through chat rooms, blogs, and e-mails as one friend introduces the browser to the next. The little details make this new Chinese browser better.

Maxthon, which is supposed to mean "maxed on," has never spent a cent on promotion. Innovative features have done the advertising for it. "Maxthon has passed a classic Internet success test, having achieved a significant following entirely through word of mouth and without any marketing spending," says the former Internet analyst Safa Rashtchy at Piper Jaffray & Co. Chen still is trying to keep his own profile low. "I want Maxthon to be famous, but not me," says Chen, who is 32 years old.

Maxthon is a good example of the flat world of global technology development, where ideas spread rapidly through instant online communications. Chen works with a small group of developers in Beijing, supported by online programmers around the world working together in open-source software code.

The idea is to speed up the pace of tech innovation with codes that are available for anyone to see, not sealed off to the public, for instance, by a commercial enterprise such as Google, Apple, or Microsoft. This is the same movement that developed the Linux operating system, a rival of Microsoft.

"Jeff is a 360 kind of guy. Very few people can get stuff done, make money, and write code, but Jeff can. He is the company."

Morten Lund,
Danish tech investor and
cofounder, LundKenner

Chen's managerial team is in Hong Kong, Palo Alto, and Copenhagen. Team members communicate primarily by Skpe, as one might expect. Without the brainy Chen in the front row, Maxthon would not have made it. "Jeff is a 360 kind of guy. Very few people can get stuff done, make money, and write code, but Jeff can," says Lund. "He *is* the company."

Although not registering among the top five most popular browsers worldwide, Maxthon claims a hefty 115 million downloads.[2] For the latest update, visit the Maxthon site, where a counter on the home page racks up downloads by the split second. Microsoft's Internet Explorer owns a dominant 81 percent share of the browser market worldwide. The only major alternative is Firefox, which trailed Maxthon in developing tab browsing, with a 13 percent share globally.[3] The once-dominant Netscape has tumbled to less than 1 percent of the global market after losing the late-1990s browser war with Microsoft.

In China, Maxthon has muscled into second place after Internet Explorer and has an estimated 30 percent market share.[4] "There's always one brand that dominates worldwide, like Coke," says Maxthon investor Lund. "But in local markets, there's a local drink that beats Coke because it delivers a local flavor."

No single start-up has the perfect formula: technology, business model, management, financials, and funding. Maxthon is no exception. It has the perennial problem that plagues nearly all young Chinese companies: lack of experience and thin management. A generation of managers who would be in their forties and fifties now was stymied by the Cultural Revolution. The innovators who are emerging today are among the first to test their skills in starting businesses. They have no older role models in private enterprise in China the way Americans have Bill Gates and Steve Jobs, who are now in their early fifties.

At Maxthon, Lund pumped up the management team in 2005 by recruiting the Swedish tech entrepreneur and former AOL executive Netanel Jacobsson. But in September 2007 Jacobsson resigned as senior vice president of business development and became the director of international development at networking site Facebook, the hottest start-up around. From his home in Israel, he traveled to Silicon Valley to build Maxthon's presence outside China. Now Jacobsson is moving his family to Palo Alto, something Maxthon did not have the resources to handle. Going forward, Maxthon's China team and a possible part-time U.S. representative will handle any potential projects with American companies, such as a strategic deal with Google that was made in spring 2007. From China, these deals are a stretch. Besides that, Chen is a geek first and a manager by happenstance. Says Lund, "I'd be lying if I said Jeff is a good manager."

Nevertheless, Jacobsson's skip to Facebook is symbolic. He is one of the first tech entrepreneurs to leap from a Chinese to an American start-up, a sign of the growing stature of made-in-China technology.

Maxthon's Chinese heritage, though advantageous on some fronts, also could be a negative. Some people might think twice before using a Chinese browser to surf the Net. What about spyware to monitor what's viewed online? What about blocked searches of politically sensitive subjects by Chinese government censors? Everyone on the small Maxthon team tells me it's not a big deal. Users in Mainland China allegedly can get past Chinese firewalls by downloading a plug-in feature to Maxthon so that their clicks on Web sites are routed to proxy servers in Canada and other overseas locations. A reflected image of the content then is beamed into cyberspace to the user's screen. It sounds like science fiction, but Maxthon investor Tai tells me, "It's pretty standard stuff these days."

Why Maxthon came from China and not the Redmond, Washington, campus of Microsoft Corp. is beyond me. The creative spirit behind Maxthon is Chen, an almost accidental entrepreneur who enjoys staying up nights writing software code.

I meet Chen at his office in Beijing's HaiDian district not far from the city's Zhongguancun Software Park. There is no listing of Maxthon in the lobby of the sleek multi-story building. I call Chen, and he directs me down a long hallway on the ground floor. There I find him, dressed Silicon Valley techie style in blue jeans and a black pullover sweater that accentuate his slim frame, standing self-assuredly in a doorway emblazoned with Maxthon's bold masculine logo. During a long interview with Chen, his eyes glazing over with fatigue, I hear how he has come so far.

The son of factory workers, Chen grew up in the dusty industrial city of Zhengzhou, the capital of China's Henan province. He's been to the United States three times, the first time in January 2006 to exhibit Maxthon at a Las Vegas electronics convention. He doesn't have a computer science or engineering degree from Stanford like a lot of the earlier Chinese tech inventors and copiers. He wasn't brought up in a free society that encourages the imaginative individualistic thinking that has inspired leading-edge innovations from Silicon Valley over the last couple of decades. Chen was so poor when he began developing Maxthon five years ago that he lived off donations from fellow software programmers working with him online.

Yet from those humble roots, by spring 2006 Chen had raised $5 million from a Who's Who of tech investors globally. Granted, he had to turn over 15 percent of Maxthon shares to the U.S. venture firm Charles River Ventures for a $2.5 million investment in May 2006 and approximately 10 percent to WI Harper for the initial $500,000 in 2005 and subsequent financing. Google has a minority stake in Maxthon from a $1 million investment in spring 2007.

Could the next step be an acquisition by Google? Maybe, but that probably won't happen too soon. Chen tells me that he has received one "serious offer" to acquire Maxthon. He turned it down because, "It is too early to sell the company." Chen confides, "I don't want to be a rich guy. I just want to make my product and use it. If the money comes, okay." He doesn't really need it. "My life is very simple. I work and rest." I've heard the same thing from most of the Chinese entrepreneurs I've interviewed.

Fortune cookie

Maxthon's business model is a work in progress. Chen claims that his young start-up has been breaking even since 2003, largely because of donations. He prefers not to pinpoint revenues, instead hinting that big things are to come.

"Since change always happens, we cannot really predict a number. And we don't want the public to have a number in mind to limit their imaginations. So we'd rather not to say any number," he tells me.

"We don't want the public to have a number in mind to limit their imaginations."

Jeff Chen,
founder and CEO, Maxthon

And talk about luck. Chen has it. Besides hooking up with one of the world's most famous tech investors and getting free development help and financial support from programmers online, he has what every entrepreneur desires more than anything else: a supportive and hip-looking wife, Carol, who works alongside him in the growing business and makes sure he remembers to eat and sleep. Carol lives in Hong Kong but comes often to Beijing to fill in as chief financial officer and human resources manager for the 30-employee firm. They met through a mutual friend in Beijing and haven't taken a vacation together yet. Carol is so wrapped up in the business that she is recording her husband's progress in a diary she set up on MySpace.

Chen started out by earning a mechanical engineering degree in 1998 from Beijing Institute of Technology. His first job was as an engineer at the Chinese firm HanWang Corp., where he spent two years designing software that could recognize handwriting electronically for digital input. Chen got his first peek outside China—an experience that contributed to the development of Maxthon—when his employer transferred him to Singapore as a senior engineer to figure out the technology for detecting forged documents.

Chen found Singapore's greenery, lush flowers, and tropical climate enjoyable but was bored, and he took up a hobby. "As I was surfing online, I found that the browsers didn't really suit my needs, so I decided to make my own browser. It's something I'm good at and something I can share with friends," he says.

Chen picked up the original source code for the browser from a university student in Beijing who called himself Changyou. When the Falun Gong devotee Changyou posted the code on an online bulletin board system and disappeared into cyberspace, Chen, who took the name BloodChen for some mysterious and unexplained reason, took over the project, spearheading an online grassroots movement to make browsers better.

Over the summer of 2002, Chen developed a beta, or test, version of his browser software. Working with software developers online, he detected bugs or defects in his handiwork. Word spread among techies online. Soon Chen was writing codes over the Web with as many as 50 software developers. No one actually knew who Chen was. He was a virtual developer.

Maxthon grew out of a grassroots effort in the online tech community to create a viable alternative to Microsoft's Internet Explorer. Microsoft had overtaken Netscape in the late 1990s with tactics that sparked a headline-grabbing antitrust suit when it pre-installed Internet Explorer browsers into the Windows 95 operating system. Microsoft was criticized openly for failing to innovate once it had market leadership. Two former Netscape workers in the United States, Dave Hyatt and Blake Ross, shepherded a nonprofit group, Mozilla.org, that rolled out the alternative browser Firefox in 2004. At about the same time Firefox emerged, on the other side of the Pacific Ocean Chen was hunched over his computer writing code for what became Maxthon.

Both Maxthon and Firefox came with lots of built-in functions for easy and personalized surfing on the Web. The main difference is that Firefox has Netscape as its rootstock, whereas Maxthon is built on the same code used in

Internet Explorer. "I'm still using Maxthon out of dogged loyalty," says Kuo, now group director for digital strategy at Ogilvy China. "Truth is, if you set up Firefox right, you can do most of what Maxthon does."

Little more than five years ago Chen got by on $2 to $5 contributions from the PayPal account he set up. By 2004, the amounts grew to hundreds of thousands of dollars. Chen quit his day job and began devoting all but his sleeping and eating hours to the project.

After raising his first big bucks in 2005, Chen set up shop in his investor's office and hired a few techies to do more tests of the software. Soon, with 15 employees, he leased space on the outskirts of Beijing, where the air quality was better and the surroundings more peaceful. It wasn't long before Chen's team perfected the browser, tellingly called MyIE2, a reference to the Microsoft browser. Chen later changed the name to Maxthon to avoid confusion with Internet Explorer.

In effect, Maxthon is both a partner of and an indirect competitor of Internet Explorer. Because Maxthon has been developed with support from the open source community, Microsoft can gauge what features are most popular and then pick them up to use in Internet Explorer. The latest version of Internet Explorer, released in 2006, incorporates several features originally offered by Maxthon.

Donations from developers and venture capital still help with many of Maxthon's expenses. The $1 million strategic deal with Google China could bring in additional revenues from paid searches directed from the Chinese browser to the American search engine. Maxthon has begun to feed online searches to Google in China, making a switch from Google's China rival Baidu. In return, Maxthon is working with Google to increase its presence in the United States, though the business details were not disclosed to me.

Other potential revenue sources are distribution partnerships with Amazon and eBay. For a fee, Maxthon would display its services on the browser and then share sales revenue. More ideas include building out the browser with e-mail, calendars, contact lists, and interactive services that can be supported by advertising. "We want to monetize the service, but we don't want to make it too commercial," says Chen.

At some point soon, the Maxthon team will have to evolve the business plan. No one would blame the team for being tempted by a takeover offer from Google. After all, Google bought the then-unprofitable YouTube video download service for $1.6 billion in fall 2006 after only three meetings with YouTube's cofounders at a restaurant in Silicon Valley. I doubt Chen will let go so readily because he has so much of his soul tied up in the project. But with two venture investors owning such a large stake in his firm, Chen may be convinced that it's the right thing to do, particularly since he and his wife want to start a family. Being bought out by Google would not be the worst thing in the world, especially when Microsoft is adapting what is being developed by Maxthon and its developers.

In the next chapter, we leave the software and Internet zones to peer into the esoteric world of light-emitting diodes (LEDs). LEDs provide light that is bright and efficient. They're already being used for traffic lights and electronic gadgets and are beginning to replace the standard lightbulb. Very few companies worldwide know how to put this technology to work. Now one of them comes from China. Here, in a university laboratory in the southeastern city of Nanchang, a brilliant scientist has invented an advanced technology for making LEDs. Soon a large factory will begin cranking out the little white lights. For this we have to thank a leading Chinese scientist, Professor Jiang Fengyi, and his 15-and-growing number of patents. This may be the next $1 billion initial public offering on Nasdaq.

CHAPTER TWELVE

Leading Chinese scientist Jiang Fengyi has invented a cheaper, longer-lasting light that promises to replace incandescent and fluorescent lightbulbs, with energy savings of more than 50 percent. The next steps are to take LatticePower from the laboratory to the assembly line and ramp up for a billion-dollar IPO.

LatticePower Corporation— China Lights Up the Globe

My China Eastern Airlines flight from Beijing to Nanchang, a third-tier city in the southeast, takes only two hours. I'm here on a day trip to meet with Jiang Fengyi, a leading Chinese scientist and the country's hope for a gigantic technology breakthrough.

A modern-day Thomas Edison, Jiang has 15 patents for making lights so efficient and bright that one day they could make the ubiquitous General Electric bulb obsolete. He spends most days—and occasional nights—in a research laboratory in the Ivy League setting of Nanchang University, where he teaches physics when he is not working on his new energy-saving, long-lasting light. Jiang hopes his research will transform the century-old lighting industry radically and raise China's status from a largely poor rural country to a major contributor of cutting-edge technology. Backed by the Chinese government and $45 million from four major international investors, Jiang's start-up, LatticePower Corporation, promises to be to the world of lights what Microsoft and Intel were to information technology. If that happens, it could help China and the world solve major energy and environmental problems.

Youngish-looking at age 44, the Chinese-born and -educated scientist often is referred to as Professor Jiang because he still teaches at the large science-focused university when he is not inventing the light of tomorrow. Jiang has an Einsteinian aura but follows in the footsteps of the practical-minded inventor Thomas Edison, who would crawl into his roll-top desk, curl up, and nap after marathon work sessions.[1] Jiang nods on a cot behind a divider in his private office, often staying overnight to work in his nearby lab.

The Chinese scientist's life's work is focused on making LEDs (light-emitting diodes), which are lights charged by semiconductors. This highly specialized research is concentrated in only a handful of laboratories, institutions, and companies worldwide and includes such trailblazers as Nichia Corporation in Tokushima on Japan's main island of Shikoku and the Nasdaq-listed Cree Inc. in Durham, North Carolina.[2]

On my visit to Nanchang in May 2007, I toured the firm's new production facility, which is the size of 50 soccer fields. Sunburned construction workers resided in on-site dormitories, cows grazed in a nearby pasture, and bricks were being transported by wheelbarrow. Nanchang is one of four cities in China tapped by the government as a base for developing this new type of lighting[3] and making China—not Taiwan—the world's largest producer of LEDs. The land for building the plant, on the outskirts of town, was purchased from the government at a favorable price. Tax breaks were tossed in as incentives to turn the open acreage into a glistening high-tech development zone in Jiangxi province's capital city.

Until recently, production was limited to a single line at the university lab. To enter this secret chamber, I donned sanitized coveralls, hat, and gloves and passed through a so-called air shower to get rid of any remaining dust or particles. Once inside, I saw a digital display board lit up in LEDs, several bulky mainframe-type computers, and uniformed workers behind glass booths blending physics, chemistry, and semiconductor technology. I was not allowed to take photographs.

Jiang and his laboratory symbolize the high priority the Chinese government has placed on developing LEDs. China's Ministry of Science and Technology is spearheading a new multifaceted national LED push[4] that is budgeted at $44 million[5] to develop high tech as a pillar of economic growth[6] and help solve the nation's energy problem.[7] China is the second-largest energy-consuming nation after the United States[8] but is home to 20 percent of the world's population.[9] By 2015, savings from this Chinese lighting initiative could equal the output of the country's massive Three Gorges hydroelectric project, according to Wu Ling, the director of the national project.[10]

Globally, the LED market is set to double in size to $12.3 billion by 2012, up from $6.1 billion in 2007.[11] Today, LEDs are found most commonly in traffic lights, mobile phones, digital cameras, automotive interiors, taillights, and flashlights, soon to be followed by airplane cabins. LEDs also are replacing neon lights in outdoor advertising signs such as those in New York's Times Square, including a seven-story LED screen that wraps around Nasdaq's headquarters. It is estimated that by 2012 LEDs will account for 10 percent of the $1.8 billion lighting market in homes and offices, up from only $100 million in 2007.[12]

LEDs can decrease the amount of electricity used in lighting by more than 50 percent and reduce carbon emissions by more than 10 percent.[13] Compared with the average lightbulb, an LED bulb uses half the electricity and shines for a far longer time—even years—before burning out. The only drawback is the price: A 9.2-watt LED bulb costs $65. Jiang's research, if successful commercially, will lower prices significantly and could put LED lightbulbs in billions of lamps worldwide.

I recall my father, a professor of history at Ohio University, telling me that whoever invented a long-lasting, cool electric lightbulb would be a millionaire. I am sure he would be surprised to hear that this breakthrough is coming from a country where some rural people don't have reliable electricity and from a city outside the major commercial centers.

Despite Jiang's efforts to keep a low profile, he is known increasingly in high-tech circles in China and worldwide. Jiang has hit on a highly efficient way of making light-emitting diodes by using the commodity silicon, which is found in computers, cell phones, and digital cameras. This is breakthrough research,

"If it's true that they can make LEDs on silicon, this is really a breakthrough. This is the holy grail."

Jagdish Rebello,
technology analyst, iSuppli Corp.

not another copycat Internet start-up. But first, full-scale production must be cranked up, a test of commercialization that most labs fail.

The start-up's trade secrets are closely guarded. Even leading technology analysts such as Jagdish Rebello of the Silicon Valley research firm iSuppli Corporation are surprised to hear about it. "If it's true that they can make LEDs on silicon, this is really a breakthrough," says Rebello. "This is the holy grail of LEDs." Senior analyst Jed Dorsheimer with the Boston financial service firm Canaccord Adams doubts that LatticePower has mastered the technology. "Right now, most Chinese technology is mediocre, and it would be hard to find a leading-edge technology company," he says. "At some point in time, technology breakthroughs from China will happen. The question is when."

The investors in LatticePower are convinced that the answer is now. Ask Sonny Wu, who manages the Chinese venture firm GSR. He says that LatticePower has "the missing link to energy savings in lights." He has led three groups from the United States, Taiwan, and Singapore to invest $45 million[14] in the lighting start-up. He recently recruited a new high-powered CEO to LatticePower: Tony Liu, the former head of the publicly traded semiconductor firm ASMC,[15] and a Ph.D. from UC-Berkeley with 10-plus years of experience in China as a plant and general manager. Wu says that LatticePower is aiming for an initial

public offering, possibly by 2010, that will put high-flying publicly traded Chinese tech companies to shame. "We are not rushing it," says Wu. "We want to lead LatticePower toward a billions IPO," he says, pointedly not specifying a billion dollar amount. He adds that he's confident the firm will top out with a "market valuation of $10 billion."

I first met the scientist Jiang in November 2006 in the lobby of Beijing's five-star Grand Hyatt Hotel while the city was hosting an unprecedented China-Africa trade and investment summit that made Manhattan during the annual United Nations sessions seem calm. Jiang seemed energized, surrounded by African diplomats and having hushed conversations over coffee and tea. He spent an hour sharing his story of humble origins and his plans for commercializing his breakthrough and patented research.

China's great hope

Jiang grew up during the Cultural Revolution to the east of Nanchang in the small fishing village of Yugan, where his parents were farmers and his father was a town leader. As part of an education grounded in science, he first studied physics in middle school. He graduated in 1984 at the age of 21 with a degree in physics from Jilin University, a leading national university in the northeastern Chinese city Changchun that is known for its physics college. Jiang returned to his native region and taught physics for three years at the Jiangxi Polytechnic University, now part of Nanchang University, where today the professor works on matching up the complex crystal structures of atoms. In 1989, he received a master's degree from the research-focused Changchun Physics Institute of the Chinese Academy of Sciences. At Changchun, one of eleven branches of the prestigious academy, Jiang's graduate adviser recognized his skills at hands-on research in the lab, a talent that led 17 years later to the formation of LatticePower, which is named after a basic physics principle.

After graduation, Jiang returned to Nanchang "to be with my local people." There he nixed any thought he'd had as a boy of pursuing a career as a doctor and instead dug into his research. Jiang downplays any notion that he was inspired by China's first Nobel Prize-winning physicists Chen Ning Yang and Tsung-Dao Lee. "When I was young, I had no knowledge of them," he says. Instead, his motivation came from his professors' encouragement, but he pointedly adds that his "persistence and energy came from myself."

"My goal was low key, to take it step by step," Jiang says. "I had no huge ambition for a technology innovation or for LatticePower to become a world-class company."

Jiang took time out only to get married and raise a family and to play an occasional game of Xiangqi, or Chinese chess, a fast-moving tactical board game that exercises the brain the way Western chess does. To facilitate about a dozen governmental grants and support for his research, the Jiangxi Changda Photoelectric Technology Co. was formed with Jiang as general manager and Nanchang University as the majority owner. In February 2006, LatticePower was established, and today it has an approximately 30-member research and development team, all born and educated in China. Six of the researchers are Jiang's Ph.D. students, and the rest come from leading Chinese science universities. Jiang says his team is moving faster than comparable labs in Germany and Japan that he has visited. He is not sure about the United States. Three years ago he applied for a visa to the United States but was rejected, he says.

"I had no huge ambition for a technology innovation or for LatticePower to become a world-class company."

Jiang Fengyi,
president, LatticePower Corporation

Jiang asks me if I would like to see a demonstration of his light-emitting diodes. There in the lobby, his colleague and vice president Wang Min, who is in charge of governmental relationships, administration, and logistics support, picks up an aluminum-encased suitcase. He snaps open the clasps and opens it, and I see bright white letters in the thousands spelling out the company's name.

Jiang smiles proudly at my amazement at the show of lights. He leans over and with his intelligent-looking brown eyes asks me if I'd like a close look at the tiny lights. Opening a clear plastic sandwich bag, he takes out a clear jelly-bean-shaped object: a single LED. He holds up the fruits of his research, and I snap a quick photo before he hides it, not wanting to give away too much intellectual property in public.

Buying into the hypothesis that this is world-class disruptive technology, I ask Jiang if he wants to be famous. He instantly begs off. "Not really." Well, wouldn't it be great to turn LatticePower into a moneymaking publicly traded enterprise? He beams. "Yes, but not for myself, but for the good of society." I see that Jiang, aside from being a master scientist, is well schooled in the communist principles of building a harmonious society and of sharing wealth before making individual gains.

Tracking the milestones

LatticePower has passed several major milestones. The biggest was in February 2007, when the Chinese tech start-up broke ground for its new plant in a ceremony attended by numerous high-level government officials. Equipment has been imported, and production is supposed to start by March 2008. Some 500 employees were to be onboard by year end 2007, up from 100 in late 2006.

Revenues are projected to be $50 million in 2008 and $200 million within five years. The goal is to be profitable within two years. Initially, most of the plant's LEDs are meant for local markets, but global customers could be next. Jiang says he is confident that LatticePower will attract a multinational clientele and names the cell phone maker Nokia as one possibility.

Investor Sonny Wu[16] was tipped off in 2000 about Jiang's breakthrough research by a senior official from the Chinese government's Ministry of Information Industry. Then, in 2001, Jiang's colleague Wang Min showed a preliminary business plan to his former college classmate Alex Pan. The same year, Pan visited the scientist in Nanchang, and he and Wu, both veterans of semiconductor and telecom businesses, began tracking the scientist's research. Shortly after teaming up to establish the Chinese venture firm GSR in 2005, they invested in the LED research start-up.

Few start-ups have benefited from as much hands-on investor mentoring as LatticePower has from GSR, which is named after a part of China's mighty Yantgze called the Golden Sands River. GSR helped Jiang protect his inventions from being ripped off by obtaining international patents through lawyers at Fernandez & Associates in Menlo Park, California. Many Chinese start-ups do not appreciate the importance of putting up high barriers around research, an essential step for success in international markets.[17] LatticePower has filed for several more patents in addition to the 15 already granted.

Attorneys were hired to form LatticePower in early 2006 as a Cayman Islands corporation to facilitate two-stage venture capital financing of $10 million followed by $35 million[18] and a possible listing of the firm on an overseas exchange. Additionally, four MBA students were packed off to

Nanchang to work for a summer on developing financial projections for the start-up business.

Advice was solicited from Richard Chang, president and CEO of the Shanghai-based and NYSE-listed Semiconductor Manufacturing International Corp. Chang, who has overseen the development of an impressive production facility and nearby community for his employees, spent two days in Nanchang, offering tips on everything from safety issues to building on-site housing for workers like the one SMIC has in Shanghai's Pudong industrial area.

After an eight-month search, another building block was put in place with the hiring of new CEO Liu. The experienced business manager Liu supplements the research talents of Jiang, who is president of the firm. GSR's Wu says it was difficult to find a well-qualified candidate who would work in Nanchang, a modern city of nearly 2 million people but off the beaten path for most international executives. Luckily, it was easier to find a qualified candidate as board secretary and finance manager, Sophia Liu, a native of Nanchang. She recently returned to her hometown to join the research start-up after working in the venture business in Silicon Valley for many years.[19]

Lattice mismatch

Professor Jiang is concentrating on the highest end of LED production: blue LEDs, the most difficult color to produce and the key technology for making white light.[20] Only a handful of firms can make blue LEDs, Cree[21] and Nichia included.[22]

The trick in making such high-performance LEDs is to match up the crystal lattice structures of two different semiconductor materials precisely at the level of a nanometer (one-billionth of a meter). Each group uses different materials: LatticePower works with silicon, and Nichia with the far more expensive sapphire, whereas Cree uses silicon carbide, a compound of silicon and carbon. If it is successful in mass-producing LEDs with the widely available silicon, LatticePower will have a significant cost advantage. But analyst Jed Dorsheimer has his doubts that LatticePower will succeed with silicon. "None of the companies I have seen so far have been able to achieve commercial production at a reasonable performance," he says.

As recently as 2002, China imported all its high-performance chips for LEDs, and the emerging domestic industry supplied only 5 percent of demand in 2003.[23] But China has big ambitions, points out Robert Steele, director, LED practice at the market research firm Strategies Unlimited in Silicon Valley. "China expects to be the largest market for LEDs and solid-state lighting in the world," he says.

Currently, Taiwan supplies about 50 percent of the global LED market, followed by Japan and South Korea, with China at about 5 percent.[24] Most packaging for LEDs is done in China[25]—grunt work compared with the high-tech artistry of making bright white LED lights, in which China is outpaced by the United States, Japan, and Europe. "Chinese companies have failed to make an impression with high-performance chips," says Tim Whittaker, editor of *LEDs* magazine.

Taiwan, the world's largest semiconductor producer and home to the two top foundries globally,[26] has a natural base for making LEDs. China does not have that history of making high-volume and low-cost semiconductors, says analyst Steele. "But they're smart people. They'll figure it out in maybe three to five years."

They already are figuring it out. Today, the skyline in Xiamen on the east coast of China, right across the Taiwan Strait, is ablaze in a dazzling rainbow of lights powered by domestically produced LEDs. A landmark bridge in China's third largest city, Tianjin, is lit with bright LEDs that change colors in sync with shooting fountains of water above steel arches. Both sights symbolize China's fast embrace of tomorrow's technologies, whether wireless communications, software, or lighting.

LatticePower is setting a new paradigm for China's status as an inventor—not a manufacturer or nimble replicator—as the twenty-first century unfolds. Now as China awakens, expect to see more Chinese technology breaking barriers, shifting the balance of power, and changing the world as we know it.

> "China expects to be the largest market for LEDs and solid-state lighting in the world."
>
> **Robert Steele,**
> director, LED practice,
> Strategies Unlimited

ENDNOTES

Introduction

1. Tudou's investors in May 2006 included Granite Global Ventures, JAFCO Asia, and IDG Technology Venture Investments. Helen Wong is a partner at Granite Global.

2. Silicon Valley owes much of its recent innovation boom to Chinese and Indian citizens, who have accounted for nearly one-third of the region's start-ups since the 1980s, according to a study by the dean and professor AnnaLee Saxenian at the University of California, Berkeley.

3. Heidrick & Struggles partnered with the Stanford Project on Regions of Innovation and Entrepreneurship in an 18-month study of leadership skills at Chinese high-tech companies. The study was released in November 2006.

4. Duke School of Engineering. Some experts claim that China uses a broader definition of these categories and thus the Chinese numbers are inflated. Even by a narrower definition, China has the lead.

5. Additionally, some 112 Chinese start-ups, or more than one-third of all Asian deals, got venture capital in 2006, up from 54 in 2005, according to the Hong Kong weekly *Asian Venture Capital Journal*. China has been the world's fastest-growing venture market for several years but remains tiny compared with the dominant U.S. market.

6. U.S. venture investment inched up 8 percent to $26 billion in 2006 and chalked up $14.2 billion in the first half of 2007. This compares with 2,454 U.S. companies in 2006 and 1,319 in the first half of 2007, according to Ernst & Young/VentureOne.

7. China Internet/Media report, Morgan Stanley Equity Research, April 12, 2007.

8. GSR Ventures' analysis based on data from Piper Jaffray and VentureOne. Market capitalization is based on the trading price at the end of 2005.

9. The source for the mobile phone figure is China's Ministry of Information Industry as of June 2007. The Internet figure is from the China Internet Network Information Center as of June 2007. Global ranking of Web sites is from Alexa Internet Inc.

10. China's Impact on the Semiconductor Industry, PriceWaterhouseCoopers 2006 Update.

11. Saffo, a fellow at the Institute of the Future, is on sabbatical, doing research and teaching at Stanford, where he is a consulting associate professor in the School of Engineering.

12. The source is the World Intellectual Property Organization, "The International Patent System in 2006," *PCT Yearly Review*. In 2005, China also had the world's fastest growth rate for new patent filings, up 43 percent to 2,452, according to WIPO. In 2006, the United States had a 34 percent share of patent applications globally. Measured by patent grants, China moved up two notches to rank sixth, behind Japan, the United States, the Republic of Korea, Germany, and France.

13. Dr. Kuhn is an adviser at Citicorp and also the author of *The Man Who Changed China: The Life and Legacy of Jiang Zemin*. He noted that change is being ushered in by a new generation of officials schooled in economics and will be reinforced by the opening of the educational system to private ownership within a few years.

14. Suntech's original backers included the Chinese venture firm DragonTech Ventures.

15. The world ranking is from *Forbes*, "The World's Billionaires," May 8, 2007. China's ranking is from *Forbes*, "The 400 Richest Chinese," November 2, 2006.

16. Professor Shenkar authored a book called *The Chinese Century*.

17. The source is Bain & Co.

18. Tudou raised $18 million in April 2007 from Capital Today, General Catalyst Partners, KTB Network, and return investors JAFCO, IDG Technology Venture Investment, and Granite Global Ventures.

Chapter One

1. This statistic is from the San Francisco-based market research service Alexa Internet Inc., which measures Web page views, or the number of times users look at a particular page on a site.

2. The China Internet Network Information Center reports that China has 162 million Internet users compared with the United States at 211 million as

of June 2007. The Chinese Internet Center forecasts that Chinese Internet users will exceed U.S. users by 2009. The U.S. research firm eMarketer reports China at 156 million and the United States at 185 million in 2007. Forecast numbers in the text for China and the United States are from the U.S. research firm eMarketer.

3. Online advertising in the United States will top $35 billion by 2012, up from nearly $20 billion in 2007, predicts the industry tracker Jupiter Research. Paid searching in the United States will hit $10 billion by 2009, forecasts the research firm eMarketer, up from $8.2 billion in 2007.

4. The venture investors were DFJ ePlanet Ventures, a former global affiliate of Draper Fisher Jurvetson, and IDG Ventures China, an early investor in China and an arm of the large technology publisher and research firm IDG Group.

5. Google picked up the idea for a commercial search firm Overture Services in Pasadena, which was acquired by Yahoo! in 2003.

Chapter Two

1. Alibaba.com claims a market share in China of more than 69 percent, according to the Beijing-based Analysys International, China B2B Market Quarterly Tracker Q1 2007.

2. Some of them are eBay power sellers who resell the Chinese-made goods.

3. In 1999, Ma raised $5 million from Goldman Sachs and a few Chinese venture investors. He raised $20 million in 2000 from the Japanese Internet player Softbank Corp. In 2004, he raised $82 million from Softbank, Fidelity Ventures, Venture TDF China, and Granite Global Ventures.

4. eBay entered China in 2002 by investing $30 million for a 33 percent stake in Eachnet. In 2003, eBay acquired the remaining shares in Shao's start-up for $150 million.

5. Shao is the founder of the Chinese infant care site BabyTree.com and the drug producer and marketer NovaMed Pharmaceuticals.

6. With the $1 billion from Yahoo!, Ma bought out his venture investors in a deal that valued Alibaba at an improbable $4.1 billion. Yang and Softbank

CEO Masayoshi Son remained on Alibaba's board. Ma and his team had an 18 percent stake, Yahoo! has 40 percent, and Softbank had 16 percent.

7. Information technology consultancy iResearch in Shanghai, July 2007, market report.

8. China Center for Information Industry Development Consulting, market report.

9. Estimates for retail or business-to-consumer (B2C) e-commerce in China range widely, from $955 million in 2007, according to the Beijing market research firm Analysys International, to a same-year estimate of $2.5 billion by Shanghai's Internet market research firm iResearch.

Chapter Three

1. *China Statistical Yearbook 2005.*

2. Association of American Book Publishers.

3. 2006 annual report of China's Book Publishing market.

4. The Beijing market research firm Analysys International predicted that retail or business-to-consumer e-commerce would top $955 million in 2007, and the Shanghai market research firm iResearch estimates this Chinese e-commerce segment at $2.5 billion for 2007. The U.S. figure is an estimate from the market research firm eMarketer.

5. Analysys International, China B2C Market Quarterly Tracker, Q1 2007.

6. The couple's work was funded by International Data Group, a Boston-based technology publisher and the creator of the Dummies series of how-to books, and Luxembourg Cambridge Holding Group, a professional publisher that specializes in databases of books in emerging countries.

7. Investors included the Tiger Technology Fund. Dangdang also received investment money from the Chinese software firm Kingsoft Corp.

8. The investors were Doll Capital Management, Walden International, and Alto Global Investment.

Chapter Six

1. Blogging hosts must agree to monitor and censor blogs on their sites to filter out posts with software that blocks potentially sensitive words or subjects

that might pose a danger to national security. Posts about the spiritual group Falun Gong, Tibetan independence, and the Tiananmen Square student uprising lead to an error message or are turned into gibberish, for instance.

2. The source for the China statistics is the Internet Society of China, 2006 report. The sources for the U.S. statistics are the *Blog Herald* and the blog tracker Technorati as of April 2007.

3. Microsoft has been criticized for censoring its Chinese-language blogs on its MSN Spaces by removing words such as *freedom* and *democracy*. In early 2006, Microsoft took down an edgy politically oriented blog written by the journalist Zhao Jing, according to the media expert Rebecca MacKinnon. Microsoft said it was acting at the request of Chinese authorities.

4. Her Chinese blog was shut down in 2005, when Muzimei released the names of her sex partners. She then shifted her blog to a Chinese-language site in the United States. Her notoriety also helped her land a job as Bokee's marketing strategy manager, where her role is to publicize the merits of blogging to China's vast population.

5. The source is Technorati as of May 2006.

6. Rieschel invested in Bokee when he was the managing director at Mobius Venture Capital before he founded Qiming Ventures in Shanghai.

7. The $10 million in funding came from three American venture capital firms: Granite Global Ventures, Mobius Venture Capital, and Bessemer Venture Partners in addition to Softbank Asia Infrastructure Fund, a partnership between Japan's Softbank and the U.S. computer networking giant Cisco Systems.

8. In May, the government backed down and decided that it would be all right for bloggers to provide only an e-mail address and an anonymous user identification name. But in late August new guidelines issued by the Internet Society of China encouraged blog providers to ask users to register their real names and contact information. Bloggers also were asked to delete "illegal and bad" comments from their posts. Sohu, SINA, Yahoo! China, and Microsoft have agreed to follow the new guidelines, according to an AP report and Reporters without Borders.

9. Formula 1 race car coaches posted blog diaries about race car training, and Bokee users were invited to participate in a Q&A racing contest with prizes awarded to the winners. Tan says Ford got 1,200 prospective buyers out of the push, which also helped to build Bokee's base of users.

Chapter Seven

1. Sequoia's most recently raised U.S. fund totaled $860 million.

2. Global venture capital investments hit $32 billion in 2006, the highest level since the dot-com boom of 2001, according to VentureOne and Ernst & Young.

3. The source for China fund sizes and numbers of investments is *Asian Venture Capital Journal*.

4. U.S. venture funds hit $24.7 billion in 2006. The source for U.S. fund sizes and numbers of investments is Dow Jones Venture One.

5. China accounted for more than one-third of the 307 Asian companies that got venture financing in 2006. The source is *Asian Venture Capital Journal*.

6. In the United States, there were 2,441 venture financings in 2006 and 2,307 in 2005, according to Dow Jones Venture One. These numbers include venture capital from seed rounds to later-stage financing.

7. Bolstered by two megadeals, Chinese company initial public offerings (IPOs) raised the world's most capital at $56.6 billion in 2006, followed by U.S. companies at $34.1 billion. China also chalked up the world's largest IPO ever, the $22 billion raised from the nation's largest state-owned bank, Industrial Commercial Bank of China. Tech IPOs from China are not shabby either. Eight Chinese tech firms that went public in 2006 raised a combined $6.3 billion on Nasdaq and the New York Stock Exchange.

8. The source is *Venture Capital Journal*.

9. The source is EMAlternatives, an advisory firm for institutional investors.

10. With the new stiffer requirements and higher fees for listing a company on Nasdaq and the New York Stock Exchange, the lower-profile Hong Kong Stock Exchange has emerged as an alternative.

Chapter Eight

1. Research is from International Data Corp.

2. The forecast is from the industry expert Telematics Research Group.

Prices for installed GPS systems range from $1,200 to $2,500, according to Telematics, and portable devices cost $200 to $400.

3. In Europe, 15 percent of cars have navigation equipment; the percentage for North America is 8 percent, according to the British research firm Canalys.

4. The United States had 1.3 million navigation-tooled cell phones and PDAs in 2006, according to Telematics Research Group.

5. Location services built for GPS-equipped phones is another growth area. This market will climb from $1 billion in 2007 to more than $8.5 billion by the end of 2010, with Asia leading in growth, followed by North America and Europe, according to the telecom analyst firm Juniper Research.

6. Both mapmakers have been in business for more than two decades and are publicly listed, TeleAtlas on the Frankfurt Stock Exchange and Navteq on the New York Stock Exchange. TeleAtlas was forecasting revenues of $440 million in 2007, and Navteq was shooting for revenues of $795 million.

7. In a sign of the growing importance of navigational phones, cell phone maker Nokia agreed in October 2007 to acquire Navteq for approximately $8.1 billion. Just a few months before, in August 2007, TomTom, the world's largest maker of car navigation devices, announced that it planned to buy TeleAtlas for $2.7 billion.

8. Navteq partnered with the local operation NavInfo to form NAV2, and TeleAtlas signed an agreement with Beijing Changdi Mapping Technologies to license and distribute the domestic firm's maps.

9. Both eDuShi and City8 have won honors in the *Red Herring* Asia 100 annual tally of the region's top innovators.

10. The deal with Lingtu was not entirely straightforward. Gobi first had to buy out state-run Beijing Venture Capital Corp., which had backed Lingtu with $1 million in the early days.

11. Japan's mobile communications company NTT DoCoMo was an investor.

12. The investors were the Silicon Valley firms Sierra Ventures and Oak Investment Partners and the New York-based global asset management firm AllianceBernstein.

Chapter Nine

1. The source is Informa Telecoms & Media in London.

2. The source is iResearch in Shanghai.

3. The source is 21 Communications in Shanghai.

4. The source is Juniper Research.

5. The source is the Chinese tech market researcher CCID Consulting.

6. China has its own homegrown 3G standard called TD-SCDMA and does not use the competing standards from the United States and Europe.

7. In 2006, Oriental Wisdom churned out $3.2 million in revenues and $60,000 in profits.

8. The product ideas are suggestions from Geoffrey Handley, a director at the mobile marketing agency The Hyperfactory in China.

9. She backed both Robin Li of Baidu and Jack Ma of Alibaba.

10. Prevalent in China, BREW-designed services have been downloaded by as many 3.4 million wireless phone subscribers on 130 mobile phone models for some 43 million applications or uses since 2004, when BREW began to gain momentum, according to Qualcomm. Globally, software developers have rung up more than $1 billion in worldwide sales from products and services that use BREW, which became available in 2001.

Chapter Ten

1. The source is CCID Consulting, a Chinese information technology market research and consulting company.

2. The source is CCID Consulting.

3. PingCo has boldly—some might say foolishly—bypassed this powerful Chinese phone network by going over a channel commonly known as General Packet Radio Service (GPRS) for transmitting e-mail, data, and short-text messages over wireless connections.

4. The country's distant second-running mobile operator, China Unicom, also entered the race in early 2007 with a Shanghai tryout of its competitive service, Chao Xin.

5. In the first year, revenues were measured in monthly cycles: $2,000 in June 2006, $5,000 by September, and then $200,000 in October.

6. The venture capital was raised from initial investors GSR and Mayfield plus DCM. PingCo also got the well-regarded DCM partner Hurst Lin, the former CEO of the Nasdaq-listed SINA Corp., to join its board.

Chapter Eleven

1. This was Tai's first deal in Asia since a Web-hosting start-up, iAsiaWorks, he spearheaded went bust in the dot-com fallout and pieces were sold to competitors.

2. As of October 2007.

3. The source for market-share data is the Amsterdam-based Web analytics firm OneStat.com.

4. The estimate is from Maxthon.

Chapter Twelve

1. Edison had 1,000 patents and invented everything from the phonograph and the lightbulb to the stock ticker and the peephole viewer.

2. Cree was formed in 1987 by researchers from North Carolina State University and is headquartered in the research and development hub Research Triangle Park.

3. The other three are Xiamen, Dalian, and Shanghai. A fifth base is under development in Shenzhen.

4. The National Solid-State Lighting Program has assembled 15 research institutions and university labs and more than 2,500 companies in all segments, including packaging, components, and instruments.

5. The source is *LEDs* magazine.

6. The initiative is part of the government's new five-year economic plan, which began in 2006.

7. The solid-state lighting initiative encourages public-private partnerships and has the backing of the highest levels of the Chinese government. Support

comes from the Ministry of Science and Technology and the Ministry for Information Industries as well as the Chinese Academy of Sciences.

8. Additionally, China's per capita energy consumption is still only one-eighth that of the United States, according to the U.S. Department of State.

9. Almost all of China's oil is imported, and its power is generated primarily by domestically produced coal, which has contributed to severe air pollution in many cities. Progress is being made in meeting the country's ambitious plans to quadruple its total GDP by 2015 but only double its energy consumption. The source is *LEDs* magazine.

10. Such efforts compare to the recently passed energy bill in the United States that allocated up to $50 million annually through the Next Generation Lighting Initiative. The U.S. Department of Energy also has funded solid-state lighting research.

11. The source for these statistics is iSuppli Corp.

12. The source for these statistics is iSuppli Corp.

13. The source is the Web site for solid-state lighting supported by the U.S. Department of Energy.

14. GSR spearheaded a $10 million coinvestment in April 2006 with Asian-U.S. stalwarts Mayfield Fund of Menlo Park and AsiaVest Partners of Taiwan, followed in June 2007 by $35 million with the Singapore government's high-powered investment group Temasek Holdings as an additional investor.

15. Liu took ASMC public on the Hong Kong Stock Exchange in April 2006.

16. Wu was a cofounder of Asia Wireless Technology Group and an executive for the telecom equipment manufacturer Nortel Networks.

17. Filing patents abroad is essential if Chinese companies are to compete in international markets.

18. Board seats for LatticePower went to GSR's Wu and Pan, along with John Stockton of Mayfield Fund and Peter Hsieh of AsiaVest Partners.

19. She also continues to advise a U.S. venture fund of funds.

20. LatticePower also is working on green LED chips but not yet red LEDs, which are the hardest to make with GaN technology.

21. In March 2007, Cree gained access to the Chinese market by acquiring the privately held Cotco Luminant Device of Hong Kong for $200 million. The deal provides it with a low-cost manufacturing base.

22. Both Nichia and Cree claim on their Web sites that they invented the world's first blue LED chips.

23. The source is *LEDs* magazine, citing a speech by SSL Director Wu Ling.

24. The figure for China is from Robert Steel of Strategies Unlimited.

25. The source is IntertechPira Corp.

26. The two top foundries are Semiconductor Manufacturing Co. and United Microelectronics Corp., both in Taiwan.

Acknowledgments

No book is a solo effort. This book would not have been possible without the help of several key individuals who contributed to the process of researching and writing *Silicon Dragon*—and without good friends who provided moral support.

My editor at McGraw-Hill, Leah Spiro, has been a constant cheerleader, starting two years ago when we began to discuss the idea for this book. Leah, you know I couldn't have done this without you! Your guidance has been invaluable.

Dan Schwartz provided the entrepreneurial environment that was central to developing this book. Dan, I appreciate your understanding, and the support of the entire publishing group at *Asian Venture Capital Journal*—in Hong Kong (Allen, Harmony, Paul, Vincent), Beijing (Ying) and London, home to *AVCJ*'s new parent company, Incisive Media (Jonathon, James). And I mustn't slight my colleagues at Qiosk on Manhattan's W. 35th St., (Pat, Scott, Rebecca and Louis), who have been great office mates.

My career as a journalist and now, as a first-time book author, would never have progressed without a grounding at Ohio University and the encouragement of editors I have had the privilege of working with: Bill Holstein, who was my editor at *Chief Executive* magazine; *Jan Alexander*, the features editor at *Worth* magazine; Ed Paisley, the former managing editor at *The Deal*, Alain Sherter, editor of *Tech Confidential*, Laurel Wentz of *Ad Age*, and Rick Schine, senior editor, *Inc.* magazine. I'd also like to thank my former editors at *Red Herring*—Jason Pontin, Rafe Needleman and Michael Fitzgerald—for sending me out of the office and overseas in search of venture stories not yet reported. David Moore, I will always fondly remember the years I worked with you in the early 1990s at *International Business* magazine. You first sent me to Hong Kong in 1992 on a reporting trip, and I haven't stopped going to Asia since then!

This book would never have seen a beginning without the coaching and insights of several crucial sources: David Chao, Jim Breyer, Jenny Lee, Lip-Bu Tan, Ta-lin Hsu, Peter Mok, Henry Wong, Kyung Yoon, Tina Ju, Jixun Foo, Richard Lim, Sonny Wu, Kevin Fong, Bill Tai, Len Baker, Eric Li, Joel Kellman, Hugo Shong, Tim Draper, and Gary Rieschel. These venture capitalists, among others, helped to introduce me to the tech revolution that is unfolding in China.

They provided introductions to several Chinese entrepreneurs who are profiled in this book. Many of these Chinese up-and-comers are not accustomed to western press, but they answered questions with grace and humility. Go down the list of protagonists—Gary, Robin, Jack, Peggy, John, Joe, Xingdong, Ningzhe, "King," Charles, Jeff and Fengyi. All of you were an inspiration to me for your dedication, commitment, persistence and passion. Thanks for the time you shared with me to tell the readers of *Silicon Dragon* your entrepreneurial stories.

I also wish to acknowledge the numerous consultants, industry experts and analysts who answered endless emails and phone calls with queries about the diverse market sectors covered in these chapters. Duncan Clark, Jeremy Goldkorn, Tangos Chan, Robert Steele, Richard Ji, Jed Dorsheimer, Mark Natkin, Rebecca MacKinnon, Dave Sonnen, Tim Whittaker, Mary Meeker— thanks for explaining some of the more esoteric industry terms to me.

Writing a book is a journey. *Silicon Dragon* saw many ports. Interviews took place in tech hotspots around the globe: Silicon Valley, Shanghai, Beijing, Hong Kong and Singapore were frequent stops. This sort of 'round the world writing expedition would not have been possible before the Internet, cell phone and laptop computer.

Much of the first half of the book was written while I was on the go during a long winter. I traveled large areas of California—Rancho Santa Fe, Napa Valley, Monterey, La Jolla, Morgan Hill, San Jose, San Francisco, Sacramento, Santa Cruz, San Luis Obispo—during the initial drafting of the manuscript. These places provided a tranquil spot for turning my interviews into narratives. A special thanks goes to CordeValle and its writer's retreat, and wineries too numerous to mention. These beautiful surroundings were a welcome change after several exhausting reporting missions in mainland China. Then, it was to Connecticut and our colonial home to finish the chapters in a last four-month sprint in the summer months. At times, the leafy "Nature Center" down the road and its cows, pigs, horses and llamas, were my only companions—not to mention the frogs in the close by pond!

Next it was early fall, and on to the copy editing and production of the book. Here, thanks must go to the talented editorial assistant Morgan Ertel, the skillful copy editor Eric Lowenkron, and the efficient production mana-ger, Cheryl Hudson. I would also like to thank the McGraw-Hill marketing and public relations team for *Silicon Dragon* for their support: marketing manager Seth Morris, publicist Kenya Henderson, national account manager, Amazon.com Richard Callison, and from Hong Kong, sales manager Tamie Sung.

The finish line for this book—proofing the pages for any final revisions— was reached in Hainan Island during a tiring Thanksgiving weekend. Known as the Hawaii of China, Hainan is a copy of the American island resort, just like *Silicon Dragon* startups Tudou, Baidu, ChinaCars and Eachnet mimic YouTube, Google, the AAA and eBay. It turned out to be an appropriate finale, marked by fireworks that sounded as loud as dynamite and lit up my room from a nearby celebration on the beach.

I was warned by colleagues that writing a book is a "labor of love." Yes, it is a lot of work—and it involves sacrifice, not just for the author but for the author's loved ones.

My family backed me up in the U.S. From small-town Ohio, mom, you were always there, asking, "What chapter are you on now?" Thanks, too, to Kelly and Kyle in Columbus and Deborah and Tom in Chicago, and my relatives scattered throughout Ohio. And, how can I forget my brother Bret, who was an inspiration for my writing this book, and my father, a professor at Ohio University. From New York City, my husband John Delmar, an intellectually gifted attorney, proved to be the steady and guiding force I have counted on for years. He read and reviewed drafts, and offered just the right amount of feedback.

Thanks to each one of you for your patience, and for giving me the space to turn my dream into reality.

Rebecca A. Fannin
November 28, 2007

INDEX

A

AAA (American Automobile Association), xi, 45–47, 54
Accel Partners, xi, 67–68, 90, 94, 96
Acquire Media Corp, 8
Adaptive Broadband, 53
ADC China and Telecom Equipment, 53
Adidas, xix
Advertising and other revenue producers
    Baidu, 7, 121
    Bokee, 79
    Chinacars Inc, 51, 54
    Maxthon, 139, 141–142
    on mobile phone, 115
    Oak Pacific Interactive, 59–60
    Oriental Wisdom, 120–121
    PingCo, 131
    (*See also* Venture capital investment)
Akamai Technologies, 11–12
Alibaba China, 21
Alibaba College, 22
Alibaba Group, 23, 31
Alibaba International, 21
Alibaba.com, xvi, 19–22, 24, 26–31, 88
Alimama, 22
AliPay, 22
Alisoft, 22
Altec Industries, 65–66
AlwaysOn, xvii, 71, 75, 80
Amazon-Joyo.com partnership, 34–36, 41–43
Amazon.com, xiii, 24, 33–36, 38–41, 43, 79, 141
Analysys International, 7
Anderson, Tom, 60
Apple Computer, 105, 136
Apple iPhone, 124
AsiaInfo Holdings, xvi, 52, 60, 96
ASMC Ltd., 146
Autobytel. com, 48
AutoNavi Software Co., 108

B

Baidu, 3–18, 43, 62, 86, 88, 141
Baker, Len, x, 94, 97
Baring Private Equity Asia, 96
Barnes & Noble, 34, 36
BDA China, 63
BDA Consulting, 117, 128
Beijing Book Store, 33–34, 37
Beijing Bookworm, 37
Beijing Foreign Language Institute, 38

Beijing Institute of Technology, 140
Beijing Lingtu Software Co. (See Lingtu)
Beijing Oriental Wisdom Technology Development Co., Ltd., xv, 113–122
Beijing Summer Olympics (2008), 43, 45, 53, 72, 102, 115–116
Beijing Union University, 128
Beijing University, x, 6, 8, 10, 15, 38
Berkshire Hathaway, 69
Bertelsmann, xix
Bezos, Jeff, 24, 34–35, 38–39, 42–43, 69
Billing and payment methods, 22, 39–40, 125, 129, 131
Bird's Nest, 45
Blackberry, 106
Blogbus, 76
BlogChina, 73
BlogCN, 80
BlogDriver, 74, 77
Blogging and Bokee, 15, 71–81, 159n8
Bloomberg, 114, 124
Bokee, 71–81
Bokee Bank, 79
Booksales at Dangdang.com, 33–43
Borders, 34, 36
Boston Consulting Group, 25
BREW wireless technology, 119
Breyer, Jim, xi, 94, 96
Brin, Sergey, 4–5, 8
Broadband Capital Partners, xvi
Brown, Dan, 33
Buck's, ix
Buffett, Warren, 61, 69
Business plans
    Baidu, 11, 13
    Bokee, 80
    LatticePower, 141, 149
    Lingtu, 102
    Maxthon, 141
    Oak Pacific Interaction, 66
    PingCo, 130
    Silicon Valley influences, ix, 66
    Wang's, 130

C

California Microwave Inc., 53
CalPERS (California Public Employees Retirement System), 88
Canaccord Adams, 146
Capital Today Group, 96
Capitalization

Capitalization *(Cont'd.)*
  Baidu and Robin Li, 4–5, 10–14
  Bokee and Fang Xingdong, 76, 80
  Chinacars Inc. and John Zhang, 48, 52
  Dangdang.com and Peggy YuYu,
    37–38, 43
  LatticePower and Jiang Fengyi,
    149–150
  Lingtu, 105, 107–109
  Maxthon and Jeff Chen, 133–134,
    138–139
  Nasdaq total, xiii
  Oak Pacific Interactive and Joe Chen,
    61–62, 65–66
  Oriental Wisdom and Liu Yingkui,
    116
  (See also Venture capital investment)
Car market, 49–50
CareStar, 106
CareXpress, 51
Carlyle Group, ix
CCTV (Chinese national television network),
  10
CDC Corp., 109
Cell phones (See Mobile phone)
Censorship, 7, 14–15, 27, 72, 135–136
Chambers, John, 10
Chan, Tangos, 16, 34–35, 47, 58, 76
Chang, Richard, 93, 150
Chang, William, 9, 17
Changyou, 140
Chao, David, xvii, 37–38, 63, 68, 96
Charles River Ventures, 90, 135, 138–139
Charles Schwab, 113
Chen, Carol, 139
Chen, Jeff (Maxthon), 133–142
  capitalization, 133–134, 138–139
  competition, 135–137, 140–142
  early life and experience, 138–140
  as innovator, xv
  management challenges, 137
Chen, Joe (Oak Pacific Interactive), 57–70
  capitalization, 61–62, 65–66
  company growth and development,
    66–70
  competition, 59–61, 69–70
  early life and experience, 57–58, 61,
    64–68
  IPO goal, 63, 70
  managerial challenges, 68–69
  as returnee, 66

Chen, Wenyan (Anny), 104
Chen, Xiaoxin, 69
Chen Ning Yang, 64
Cheng, Kevin, 117
Chengwei Ventures, 97
Chery car, 47
Chevrolet automobiles, 50
China *(See specific topics)*
China Broadband Capital Partners, 60
China Central Television, xviii
China Construction Bank, 110
China Consumer Association, 50
China Eastern Airlines, 143
China International Electronic Commerce
  Center, 24
China Life, 116, 120
China Merchant Bank, 128
China Mobile, 79, 124–126, 128–131
China Netcom Group Corp., xvi, 78
China Pages, 24
China Telecom, 24, 78, 117
China Unicom, 117
China Web 2.0 Review, 47, 58, 76
Chinacars Inc. (Chinacars.com), xi, 45–55
China.com, 109
ChinaLabs, 75–78
Chinaren.com, 61, 65–66, 69
China's Legend Capital, 67
Chinese Academy of Science, 105, 109,
  147
Chinese Association of Automobile Manufac-
  turers, 50
Chinese language and venture capital, 95–97
(See also specific entrepreneurs)
Chou, David, 52
Circuit City, 123
Cisco Systems, 4, 10, 126
City8.com, 108
Clark, Duncan, 63–64, 117, 128
Clinton, Bill, 20
Coke, 114, 137
College of Staten Island, xix
Competition
  Alibaba.com and Jack Ma, 18, 21–22,
    24–28
  Bokee and Fang Xingdong, 73–74, 76,
    80
  Chinacars Inc. and John Zhang, 48
  LatticePower and Jiang Fengyi,
    150–151
  Lingtu, 108

Maxthon and Jeff Chan, 135–137, 140–142
Oak Pacific Interactive and Joe Chen, 59–61, 69–70
Oriental Wisdom and Liu Yingkui, 116–117
PingCo and Charles Wang, 125–126, 128–130
Computerized mapping and Lingtu, 101–111
Confucius, 114
Consumer payment methods, 22, 39–40, 125, 129, 131
Corruption, xviii, 29, 89, 93
Craigslist, 57–58, 68
Creativity, xiv–xv, 126
Credit Suisse First Boston, 4
Cree Corp., 144, 150
Crickee, 129
Ctrip.com, 86
Cultural Revolution as influence
   on Jeff Chen, 137
   on Joe Chen, 64
   harmonious society, communist ideal of, xiv, 127, 149
   on Jiang Fengyi, 147
   on Lingtu mapmaking, 106–107
   on Jack Ma, 21
   on Charles Wang, 127
   and wealth, 89
   on Peggy YuYu, 3
Currency, venture capital investment, 91–92
Cyworld.com, 67, 79

D
Dalian Maritime University, 105, 109
Dangdang.com, 33–43
Danwei, 20, 48, 73
DCM, xvii, 37–38, 63, 67–68, 90, 93, 96
Debevoise & Plimpton, 26
Deloitte & Touche, 90
Deng, Wendi, 58–60
Deng Xiaoping, x, 89
DeWolfe, Chris, 60
DFJ ePlanet Ventures, 13, 86, 94
DHL, 42, 114
Ding, James, 96
Disney, 8–9
Doerr, John, 89–90, 94
DoNews.com, 67
DoPod, 106
Dorsheimer, Jed, 146, 150

Dot.com bubble and bust, ix, 11–12, 28, 40–41, 54–55, 87, 95, 128
Douban. com, 68
Doubleday, 36
Dow Jones & Co., 8
Draper, Tim, 5, 94
Draper Fisher Jurvetson, 5, 10, 90
Dreyfuss, Joel, 91
Duan, Yougping, 70
Dudu.com, 67

E
E-commerce, growth of, 20, 28, 30
E-mail, 15, 28, 124, 126, 141, 159n8
Eachnet, 20, 25
Early life and experience
   Alibaba and Jack Ma, 21, 23–24
   Baidu and Robin Li, 8–9
   Bokee and Fang Xingdong, 74–76
   Chinacars Inc. and John Zhang, 49, 53–55
   Dangdang.com and Peggy YuYu, 39, 42–43
   LatticePower and Jiang Fengyi, 147–148
   Maxthon and Jeff Chen, 138–140
   Oak Pacific Interactive and Joe Chen, 57–58, 61, 64–68
   Oriental Wisdom and Liu Yingkui, 119–120, 122
   PingCo and Charles Wang, 127–128
   returnees ("sea turtles"), x, xiii, 4, 45–48, 50–51, 66, 95
EBay, xiii, 19–21, 24–25, 41, 43, 60, 66, 141
EBay China, 25–26
EBay Motors, 48
Edison, Thomas, 143–144, 163n1
Edmunds.com, 48
Education (See Early life and experience; specific institutions)
EDuShi, 108
Einstein, 61, 64
Element Fresh, ix
Ellison, Larry, 6, 69
EMarketer, 59
Engagement Marketing, 125
English language and venture capital, 95–97
Entrepreneurs (See specific people)
Ericsson, 105
Excite@Home, 87

F

Facebook, xi, 12, 57–59, 137
Fang Xingdong (Bokee), 72–81
    capitalization, 76, 80
    competition, 73–74, 76, 80
    early life and experience, 74–76
    founding, 72–74
    IPOs, 76
    managerial challenges, 76–79
Feng, Philip, 52
Feng, Vince, 68
Fengyi, Jiang (LatticePower Corporation),
    143–151
    capitalization, 149–150
    competition, 150–151
    early life and experience, 147–148
    as innovator, xv
    IPOs, 146–147
    management, 146, 150
    as researcher, 143–146
Fernandez & Associates, 149
Fetion, 129
51ditu.com, 105–106
Firefox, 134, 137, 140–141
5q.com, 68
Focus Media, 5
Focus Ventures, 94
Fong, Kevin, 96, 126, 128–129
Foo, Jixun, 80
Ford, Henry, 50
Ford automobiles, 50, 79
Founder Group, 127–128
Four Seasons Hotel (San Francisco,
    Shanghai), xviii, 20, 88
Franklin Templeton, 116
Fu, Steven, 117

G

Gallup Consulting, 41
Garage Technology Ventures, 91
Gates, Bill, xvii, 69, 114, 133, 137
Gemplus, 128
General Atlantic, 68
General Electric, xv, 28–29, 109, 143
Georgetown University Medical School, 49
Gillmor, Dan, 75
Global Entrepreneur, 62
Gobi Partners, 102–103, 110
Goldkorn, Jeremy, 20, 48, 60, 73
Goldman Sachs, 4, 38, 48, 52, 65, 94
Gome, 123

Google, xiii, xviii, xix, 3–18, 22, 43, 103,
    108, 131, 133, 136–137, 139, 141–142
Google China (Google.cn), 14–17, 127, 141
Google Earth, 15, 103
Google Maps, 15, 103
Google's AdSense, 22, 131
GPRS (General Packet Radio Service), 163n3
GPS (Global Positioning Systems), 103–107
GPS systems and devices, 103–107
Graham, Katharine, 36
Grand Hyatt Hotel (Beijing), xviii, 74, 147
Granite Global Ventures (GGV), 48, 52, 80,
    90, 116, 122
Greenspan, Alan, 20
Grisham, John, 33
Grove, Andy, 70
GSR Partners, 126–127, 130, 146, 149
GSR Ventures, xii, 96
Gu Gee (Google China), 14–17
Guoqing, Li, 36

H

Haier, xiii, 106
Hancock, Marguerite, xvi–xvii
Handley, Geoffrey, 162n8
Hangzhou University, 80
Hanhua, Wang, 41
HanWang Corp., 140
Harmonious society, communist ideal of, xiv,
    127, 149
Harvard University, 110
Heidrick & Struggles, x
Hermsen, Mike, 88
Herschbach, Dudley, 64
Hewlett-Packard (HP), 79, 105–106, 127
Hi There, 68
Home Inns, 86
Honda automobiles, 54
Hong Kong stock exchange, 20
Hotmail, xviii, 123, 126
Hotxt, 129
H&Q Asia Pacific, xviii, 92–94
HSBC Holdings, 93
Hsu, Mark, xviii
Hsu, Ta-lin, xviii, 92–94
Huang, Bill, 117
Huawer, xiii
Huffington, Arianna, 72
Hughes Electronics Corp., xix
Hurray Holding, 63
Hyatt, Dave, 140

Hyatt Hotel (Shanghai), xviii, 94
Hylanda, 68

I

IBM, 79, 93
IDC (International Data Corp.), 60, 96, 108
IDD Enterprises, 8
IDGVC China, 60, 96
Ignition Partners, 96
Ikea, 42
India, 87
Infoseek Corp., 8–9, 17
Initial public offerings (*See* IPOs and IPO
    goals)
Inktomi, 11–12
Innovation, growth and risks, xiii–xvii, 85–94
    (*See also specific innovators*)
INSEAD, xix
Instant messaging, 125
Institute of International Relations (Beijing), 49
Institutional investment, 88
Integrity Partners, 10
Intel Corp., 10, 70, 143
Intellectual property, 86, 89, 103, 148
    (*See also* Patents)
Intercontinental Hotel (Shanghai), 9
Internet
    bubble and bust, ix, 11–12, 28, 40–41,
        54–55, 87, 95, 128
    Chinese users, xii, 7, 157n2
    mobile, 113–131
    (*See also specific applications*)
Internet Explorer, xv, 137, 140–141
IPOs and IPO goals
    Alibaba and Jack Ma, 18, 20
    Baidu and Robin Li, 5
    Bokee and Fang Xingdong, 76
    Chinacars Inc. and John Zhang, 52
    Chinese capital, 160n7
    LatticePower and Jiang Fengyi,
        146–147
    Lingtu, 102, 111
    number of, xi–xii
    Oak Pacific Interactive and Joe Chen,
        63, 70
    PingCo and Charles Wang, 130–131
    venture capital investment, 87–88,
        92–94
IResearch Consulting Group, 30, 59
ISuppli Corp., 145–146
Itochu Capital, 67

J

J. Crew, 50
Jacobsson, Natanel, 137
Jajah, 129
Jamal, Asad, 13–14
Japan, Baidu in, 17–18
J.D. Power, 47
Jeffrey, Stuart, 107
J.H. Whitney & Co., 95
Ji, Richard, 17, 26
Jiang, Sun, 107
Jiangxi Changda Photoelectric Technology
    Co., 148
Jiangxi Polytechnic University, 147
Jilin University, 147
Jinglei, Xu, 73
Jintao, Hu, xiv
Jobs, Steve, xvii, 61, 103, 105, 114, 137
John Hopkins University, xix, 49
Joyo.com, 34–36, 41–43
Ju, Tina, 28–29, 90, 116–118, 120–122
Jun, Lei, 41
Jurvetson, Steve, 10

K

Ka-shing, Li, 26
Kawasaki, Guy, 91
Kentucky Fried Chicken, 23
Kerry Center Hotel (Beijing), 133
King, Bob, 10
King, Stephen, 33
Kleiner, Eugene, 90
Kleiner Perkins Caufield & Byers, xvii, 48, 90
Kodak, 69, 126
KongZhong Corp., 66, 86
Kool-Aid, 97
Kozmo.com, 40
KPCB China, 90, 118, 121–122
Kravis, Henry, 65
Ku, Hos, 80
Kuhn, Robert Lawrence, xiv, 156n13
Kuho.com, 68
Kuo, Kaiser, 114, 135, 141
Kwan, Savio, 28–30

L

Lam, Albert, 109–110
Lancel, 42
Language and venture capital, 95–97
    (*See also specific entrepreneurs*)
Lao Tse, 114

Language and venture capital *(Cont'd.)*
    LatticePower Corporation, xv,
      143–151
    Lawrence, Fred, 53
    LEDs, 151
    LEDs and LatticePower, xv, 143–151
    Lee, Jenny, 80, 116
    Lee, Kai-Fu, 7, 14–17
    Lee, Ricky, 127–128
    Lee, Tsung Dao, 147
    Legend Capital, 48, 77, 96
    Lehman Brothers (London), 107
    Lenovo, xiii, xix, 67, 96
    Lessig, Lawrence, 75
    Leung, Vincent, 109
    Li, Eric, 97
    Li, Melissa, 10
    Li, Robin (Baidu), 3–18
      capitalization, 4–5, 10–14
      as copycat, 3–4
      early life and experience, 8–9
      vs. Google, 5–18
      IPO, 5
      local and language advantages, 4
      and Eric Xu, 9–12, 16
    Li, Yanhong, 8
    Li Zhongliang, 110
    Lin, Hurst, 96
    Lin, Richard, xii
    Lincoln, Abraham, 114
    Lincoln Mercury, 57, 69
    Ling, Wu, 145
    Lingtu, 101–111
      capitalization, 105, 107–109
      competition, 108
      for consumers, 105–106
      founding, 102, 104–105
      Global Positioning Systems (GPS) and
        devices, 103–107
      IPO goal, 102, 111
      managerial challenges, 108–110
      mapmaking skills background,
        103–105
      mission, 102–103
    Linktone Ltd., 63
    Linux, 136
    Liu, James, 67–69
    Liu, King, 113–122
    Liu, Peter, 134
    Liu, Sophia, 150
    Liu, Tony, 146, 150

Liu Bang, 114
Liu Yingkui "King" (Oriental Wisdom),
    113–122
    capitalization, 116
    competition, 116–117
    early life and experience, 119–120,
      122
    innovation, 113–116
    as innovator, xv
    managerial challenges, 117–118,
      121
Living.com, 40
Lo, Vincent, 88
Local partnering, 4, 35, 92–97
Lu, Liang, 77
Lu, Ruby, 38
Lund, Morten, 89, 133–134, 136–137
LundKenner, 89, 136
Luo Chuan, 60

M
M-commerce, 115
Ma, Jack (Alibaba), 18–31
    as business superstar, 19–20, 30–31
    competition, 18, 21–22, 24–30
    early life and experience, 21, 23–24
    as innovator, xvi, 19–28
    IPO, 18, 20
    Yahoo! China acquisition, 18, 26–28
    and Zeng Ming, 27–28
Ma Bell, 129
MacKinnon, Rebecca, 72, 80, 159n3
Managerial challenges
    Bokee and Fang Xingdong, 76–79
    Chinacars Inc. and John Zhang, 48–49
    Lingtu, 108–110
    Oak Pacific Interactive and Joe Chen,
      68–69
    Oriental Wisdom and Liu Yingkui,
      117–118, 121
    start-ups, x
Mao Tse-Tung, xvi, 21, 89
MapInHand, 106
Mapping and Lingtu, 101–111
Mapquest, 105
Marbridge Consulting Group, 5
Marco Polo, 90
Marriott Hotel (Shanghai), 28
Massachusetts Mutual Financial Group, 88
MasterCard, 123
Matkin, 25

Matrix Partners, 25
Maxthon, xv, 133–142
Mayfield Fund, 90, 96, 126, 128–130
McDonald's, 16, 106, 114
Microsoft, xv, 7, 14, 26, 60, 72, 75, 103, 114, 128, 133–134, 136–138, 140–143
Min, Wang, 148–149
Ministry of Commerce, China, 91
Ministry of Commerce and State Administration Foreign Exchange, China, 91–92
Ministry of Foreign Trade and Economic Cooperation, China, 24
Ministry of Petroleum Industry, China, 54
Ministry of Science and Technology, China, 144
Mobile phone
    Chinese users, xii, 107
    maps on, 103–104, 106
    Oriental Wisdom, xv, 113–122
    PingCo, xv, 123–131
Mobius Venture Capital, 74, 96
Moore, Alan, 125
Mop.com, 58, 60, 63, 67, 69
Morgan Stanley, 17, 26, 52
Morningstar, 114
Motorola, 41, 109
Mozilla.org, 140
MSN, 6
Murdoch, Rupert, 20, 57–60, 69
Music (MP3), 17
Muzimei, 73, 159n4
MyIE2, 141
MySpace, xiii, 57–61, 63, 139
MySpace China, 57, 59–60

N
Nanchang University, xv, 143, 147–148
Nasdaq, xi–xii, xiii, xvi, xvii, 5, 13, 39, 45–55, 62, 65–66, 70, 80, 86, 91–93, 96, 111, 144–145
Natkin, Mark, xvii, 5, 35
Navteq, 102, 107
NEA (New Enterprise Associates), 90, 92–93
NetEase.com, 80
Netscape, 9, 137, 140
Neusoft, 117
New China Life, 116
New York Life Insurance, 93
New York Times, 72
New York University, 42

New Yorker, 38
News Corporation, 58–59
Newsweek, 72
Ng, Thomas, 52
Nian, Chen, 41
Nichia Corporation, 144, 150
Nike, 12
NimBuzz, 129
Nokia, 79, 102, 123–124, 149
Nortel, 107
Northeastern University, 119
NYSE (New York Stock Exchange), xi–xii, xiii, xv, 86, 91–93, 150

O
Oak Investment Partners, 93
Oak Pacific Interactive, 57–70
Ogilvy China, 114, 141
Ohio State University, xv
Ohio University, 145
Oil of Olay, 42
Olympic Games, Beijing (2008), 43, 45, 53, 72, 102, 115–116
Oracle Corp., x, 4, 105
Oriental Wisdom Technology Development Co, Ltd., xv, 113–122

P
Pacific Insurance, 116
Page, Larry, 4–5, 8
Palace Hotel (San Francisco), 19
Pan, Alex, 130, 149
Patents, xiv, xv, 8, 106, 143, 149, 156n12, 163n1
Payment methods, 22, 39–40, 125, 129, 131
PayPal, 22, 40, 141
PDAs, maps on, 106
People's Republic of China (PRC) (See specific topics)
Perkins, Tom, 90
Perkins, Tony, xvii, 71, 75, 80
Pet.mop.com, 68
Pets.com, 40
PICA, 128–129
PingCo, xv, 123–131
Piper Jaffray & Co., 6, 136
PRC (People's Republic of China) (See specific topics)
Priceline.com, 68
PriceWaterhouseCoopers, 109

Q

Qiming Ventures, 74, 96
Qing Hua University, 9
Qingwen, Sun, 109
Qualcomm, 119

R

Ra'anana, 129
Rafsky, Larry, 8
Rand McNally, 103
Rashtchy, Safa, 6, 136
Rebello, Jagdish, 145–146
Rebtel Networks, 129
Red Herring, xvii, xix, 91, 94, 135
Redstone, Sumner, 69
Renminbi, xx, 108
RenRen.com, 58, 68
Reporters without Borders, 72
Returnees ("sea turtles"), x, xiii, 4, 45–48,
   50–51, 66, 95
Rieschel, Gary, 74, 96
Risks
   innovation, xiii–xvii, 85–94
   venture capital investment, 87–88,
      90–92, 97–98
   (*See also* Competition; *specific
      companies*)
   Rockefeller family, 88
   Ross, Blake, 140
   Rubenstein, David, ix

S

Saffo, Paul, xiii–xiv, 156n11
Salesforce.com, 114
Samsung, 79
San Jose Mercury News, 75
Sand Hill Road (*See* Venture capital
   investment)
Sandell, Scott, 92
SARS (severe acute respiratory syndrome),
   94–95, 110–111
Saxenian, AnnaLee, 155n2
Schlein, Ted, 90
Schmidt, Benno, 95
Schmidt, Eric, 13–14
"Sea turtles" (returnees), x, xiii, 4, 45–48,
   50–51, 66, 95
Search engines (*See* Baidu; Google; Yahoo!)
Seiko, 42
Semiconductor International Manufacturing
   Corp. (SMIC), xiii, 93, 150

Semiconductor manufacturing, xii–xiii
Sequoia Capital, xvii, 85–86, 89, 108
Sequoia Capital China, 12, 86
Shanda Interactive, 5
Shanghai Xin Tian Di complex, 88
Shangri-La Hotel (Hangzhou, Shanghai),
   22–23
Shao, Bo, 20, 25–26, 157n4–5
Shen, Neil, 86
Shenkar, Oded, xv, 156n16
Shihe, Zhang, 73
Shihua Financial Information, 114
Shong, Hugo, xviii
Shuixing, Lin, 41
Silicon Valley, as inspiration and capital
   source, ix–x, xvii–xviii, 11–13, 85–94
Silicon Valley Bank (SVB), 94
SINA Corp., 48, 73, 96, 117
Sina.com, 48, 93
Skype, xviii, 26, 89, 123–124, 126, 131, 133,
   136
SmartGuider, 106
SMIC (Semiconductor International Manu-
   facturing Corp.), xiii, 93, 150
SMS (subscriber identity module) messaging,
   114, 124–125, 128–130
Social networking and Oak Pacific Inter-
   active, 57–70
Softbank Asia Infrastructure Fund, 90
Softbank Corp., 76
Sohu.com, 48, 65–67, 69, 73
Sonnen, Dave, 108
Sony, xix
Soros, George, 69
Ssmop.com, 68
St. Regis Hotel (Beijing), 45
Stanford University, x, xvi, 58, 61, 65–67, 69,
   71, 75, 85–86, 88, 95, 109, 138
Starbucks, 93
Start-ups
   Alibaba.com and Jack Ma, xvi, 19–31
   Baidu and Robin Li, 3–18
   Bokee and Fang Xingdong, 72–81
   cash-flow, 52
   Chinacars Inc. and John Zhang, 45–55
   Dangdang.com and Peggy YuYu, 36–42
   domestic vs. foreign–operated, 35
   investment in, ix–xi, 86–89, 91–92,
      96–97
   LatticePower and Jiang Fengyi, xv,
      143–151

Lingtu, 101–111
Maxthon and Jeff Chan, 133–142
Oak Pacific Interactive and Joe Chen, 57–70
Oriental Wisdom and Liu Yingkui, 113–122
PingCo and Charles Wang, xv, 123–131
Silicon Valley, as inspiration and capital source, ix–x, xvii–xviii, 11–13, 85–94
(*See also* Managerial challenges; Venture capital investment)
State Administration of Foreign Exchange, China, 91
State University of New York–Buffalo, 8
Steele, Robert, 151
Stock exchanges, xi
(*See also* IPOs and IPO goals; *specific stock exchanges*)
Stock market, Chinese, xii, 115
Strategies Unlimited, 151
Subway, 62
Suntech Power Holdings, xv, 62
Sutter Hill Ventures, x, 90, 94, 97
Swissotel (Beijing), 57

T
Tai, Bill, 135, 138
Tan, Lip-Bu, 92–94
Tan, Yongquan, 77–78
Tang Ningzhe, 104–105, 109–111
Taobao, 18, 25, 27, 43
TDF Capital, 90, 116, 118, 121–122
TDF Ventures, 88
Techcrunch, 67
TeleAtlas, 107–108
Tencent Holdings, 59, 62
Tencent's QQ, 128
Texas A&M University, 10, 77
Text messaging, 120, 124–126, 129, 131
Tian, Edward, xvi, 60
Tiananmen Square uprising, 21
Time, 34, 73
Tom Online, 5, 26, 48
Tsao, Thomas, 110
Tse, Lawrence, 103–106, 108–111
Tsinghua University, x, xv, 15, 74–75, 77, 127, 130
Tsung-Dao Lee, 64
Tudou.com, ix, xviii, xix

U
UAA (United Automobile Association), 48
University of California (Berkley), 95
University of Delaware (Newark), 64
University of Hong Kong, 72
University of Maryland, 49
University of Oregon, 42
University of Texas (Austin), 66, 74
UPS, 42
Upside, xvii
UUMe.com, 58, 67–68

V
Valentine, Don, 85–86, 89, 94
Venrock, 90
Venture capital investment, 85–98
advantages and opportunities, xviii, 89–90
challenges and risks, 87–88, 90–92, 97–98
currency difficulties, 91–92
Dangdang.com, 36–38, 43
as fashionable, xviii
innovation and break–out technology, 86, 89
institutional investment, 88
IPOs, 87–88, 92–94
LatticePower, 149–150
local partnering, 92–97
Silicon Valley, ix–x, xvii–xviii, 85–94
start-ups, ix–xi, 4, 86–89, 91–92, 96–97
(*See also* Capitalization)
Venture TDF, 121–122
Verity Inc., 12
Verizon, 113
Video and video sharing
Baidu, 16
Bokee, 80
Maxthon, 141–142
Oak Pacific Interactive, 58, 67–68
PingCo, 125
Toudou, xviii–xx
Vimicro International Corp., 52
Virgin Telecom, 54

W
Wal-Mart, 33
Walden International, 92–94
Waldenbooks, 36
Walt Disney Co., 8–9

Wang, Charles (PingCo), 123–131
    capitalization, 126
    competition, 125–126, 128–130
    early life and experience, 127–128
    as innovator, xv, 123–131
    IPO goal, 130–131
    start-up, 123–126
Wang, Gary, ix, x, xviii–xx
Wang, Junxiu, 78
Wang, Lei Lei, 26
Wang Jinghong, 103
Wanxiang Group, 48, 52
Web 2.0 and Oak Pacific Interactive, 57–70
Weiding, Lu, 52
Welch, Jack, 19–20, 33, 61
Wen, Eric, 52
Wen, Xin (Kevin), 74–75, 78
Wendy's, 57, 64
Wharton, 77
Whitman, Meg, 20, 22, 24, 26
Whittaker, Tim, 151
WI Harper, 134, 139
Windows 95, 140
WOFI (wholly owned foreign investment
    structure), 91–92
Wong, Helen, ix, 155n1
World of Warcraft, 68
World Trade Organization, 37, 115
WoWar.com, 68
Wozniak, Steve, 114
Wu, Martin, 26
Wu, Sonny, 146–147, 149–150
Wu, Tiger, 128
Wuhan University, 64, 109
Www.17k.com, 125
Www.google.com, 15

X

Xi'an Jiatong University of Communications,
    75
Xiaohong, Chen, 41
Xiaonei.com, 58, 68
Xie Wen, 27
Xingdong, Fang (See Fang Xingdong
    (Bokee))
Xinhua news agency, 37
Xishu, 37
Xooyo, 37
Xu, Eric, 9–13, 16–17
Xu, Kathy, xviii, 96–97

Y

Yafu, Sun, 109
Yahoo!, xiii, xvi, 3, 6, 9, 11, 14, 17, 19,
    22–24, 26–27, 41, 60, 65, 127–128
Yahoo! China, xvi, 20, 26–28, 30
Yale University, 86
Yan, Andrew, xviii
Yang, Chen Ning, 147
Yang, Jerry, xvi, 20–22, 24, 26, 65
Yang, Nick, 65–66
Yi, Alex, 52
Yingkui, Lui "King" (See Liu Yingkui "King"
    (Oriental Wisdom))
Ymer Venture Capital, 48
Yoon, Kyung, x
YouTube, ix, xviii, xix, 6, 57–58, 67,
    141–142
Yu, Albert, 10
YuYu, Peggy (Dangdang.com), 35–343
    capitalization, 37–38, 43
    company naming, 39
    on consumer payments, 39–40
    early life and experience, 39, 42–43
    merchandise mix, 41–42
    U.S. consumer experience, 35–36

Z

Zeng Ming, 27–28
Zgmop.com, 68
Zhang, Charles, 65
Zhang, Fan, 9, 12–13, 86
Zhang, John (Chinacars Inc.), 45–55
    capitalization, 48, 52
    competition, 48
    as copycat, xi
    early life and experience, 49, 53–55
    IPO goal, 52
    managerial challenges, 48–49
    as returnee, 45–48, 50–51
    Web 2.0 technology, 47–48
Zhang, Jonathan, 52
Zhanzuo.com, 12
Zhao Jung, 159n3
Zhe, Tian, 67
Zheng He, 103
Zhengrong, Shi, xv
Zhongguancun Software Park, x, 3, 138
Zhongliang, Li, 110
Zhou, Joe, 90
Zhou, Yunfan, 65–66

About the author

Rebecca A. Fannin is the international editor of the Hong Kong weekly *Asian Venture Capital Journal* and a former international news editor at *Red Herring*. Since 1992, she has been reporting on innovation, technology, and the emerging economies in Hong Kong, Bangalore, Singapore, Beijing, Shanghai, and other major cities around the world. She also is a contributor to *Inc.*, *Chief Executive*, and *Worth*.